Python RESTful APIs

Build and Consume APIs with Ease

A Step-by-Step Guide to Creating Robust Web Services with Python

MIGUEL FARMER

RAFAEL SANDERS

Table of Content

TABLE OF CONTENTS

INTRODUCTION

Python RESTful APIs: Build and Consume APIs with Ease

In today's digital landscape, **APIs (Application Programming Interfaces)** play a pivotal role in enabling software applications to communicate with each other. Whether you're building a simple web service, connecting microservices, or integrating third-party systems, APIs are the backbone of modern application development. They allow disparate systems to talk to one another, exchange data, and perform operations remotely, making them integral to businesses and technologies worldwide.

In this comprehensive guide, **"Python RESTful APIs: Build and Consume APIs with Ease"**, we delve deep into the world of **RESTful APIs**, using the power of **Python** to build robust, scalable, and high-performance web services. Whether you're a seasoned Python developer or a beginner looking to understand the fundamentals of API design, this book offers a clear, step-by-step approach to mastering API development and consumption.

Why This Book?

APIs have evolved from simple integrations to being at the heart of modern architectures. The advent of microservices, serverless computing, and the explosion of cloud-based services has made

API development more critical than ever. As organizations increasingly rely on APIs for communication, the ability to design, implement, and consume APIs effectively becomes an indispensable skill for developers.

Despite the growing demand, many developers face difficulties in building APIs that are both **scalable** and **secure**, while still maintaining ease of use. In this book, we address these challenges directly, using **Python**, one of the most popular and versatile programming languages, to illustrate the core concepts of building and consuming APIs. Python's simplicity, flexibility, and widespread adoption make it an ideal choice for developers of all experience levels.

What You'll Learn in This Book

By the end of this book, you will have a solid understanding of the key principles and best practices for building and consuming **RESTful APIs** with **Python**. Here's what you can expect:

1. **API Basics**:
   o Understanding the fundamental concepts of APIs, including **HTTP methods**, **status codes**, and **request/response formats**.
   o The difference between **REST** and other architectural styles, such as **SOAP**, and why

RESTful APIs are the most widely used in modern web services.

2. **Python in Web Development**:

    o   A deep dive into how **Flask** and **Django**, two of the most popular Python frameworks, can be used to build APIs.

    o   Setting up your Python development environment, installing essential libraries, and working with APIs in Python from scratch.

3. **Building Your First API**:

    o   Step-by-step guides on creating your first **GET** and **POST** endpoints using **Flask** and **Django**.

    o   Handling data and ensuring that responses are returned in the most suitable format (usually **JSON**) for API consumers.

4. **Advanced Features**:

    o   **Authentication and Security**: Using techniques such as **JWT** (JSON Web Tokens), **OAuth2**, and **API keys** to secure your API.

    o   **Error Handling**: Managing and responding to errors with proper HTTP status codes and error messages.

    o   **API Versioning**: Best practices for versioning your APIs to ensure backward compatibility as your API evolves over time.

- Database Integration: Connecting your API to a SQLite, PostgreSQL, or NoSQL database to persist data and interact with it through the API.

5. **Consuming APIs with Python**:
    - Using the **requests** library to consume third-party APIs and manage requests/responses.
    - Handling errors, parsing **JSON** data, and managing query parameters to interact effectively with APIs built by others.

6. **Performance and Scaling**:
    - Strategies for **scaling** your Flask or Django application to handle **increased load** through techniques like **caching, load balancing**, and **asynchronous task queues**.
    - Using **Redis** and **Celery** to offload long-running tasks from the main application thread, ensuring that your API remains responsive even during periods of heavy traffic.

7. **API Documentation**:
    - Understanding the importance of clear and accurate **API documentation** and using tools like **Swagger/OpenAPI** to automatically generate and present interactive documentation.
    - Documenting your API effectively, providing versioning information, and making sure clients can easily understand and consume your API.

8. **Monitoring and Maintenance**:

   o Setting up logging and monitoring solutions for your API to ensure it's running smoothly and to quickly detect and respond to issues.

   o Best practices for **deprecating old endpoints**, managing the **API lifecycle**, and keeping your API up-to-date with minimal disruption to users.

Who Is This Book For?

This book is designed for developers of all experience levels who are interested in learning how to **build and consume APIs** using Python. Whether you're a **beginner** looking to grasp the fundamentals of API design or an **experienced developer** seeking to improve your knowledge of advanced topics like authentication, error handling, and performance optimization, this book will provide you with the tools and knowledge you need.

- **Beginners**: If you're new to Python or API development, you'll find a friendly and comprehensive approach to learning. You'll start with the basics and progressively build your knowledge as you move through the chapters.

- **Intermediate Developers**: For those with some experience in Python, this book will offer more in-depth discussions and practical examples to help you enhance your skills, such as securing APIs, integrating with databases, and working with third-party services.

11

- **Advanced Developers**: If you're already familiar with API development, this book will allow you to dive deeper into **scaling** your APIs, handling complex tasks, and integrating cutting-edge tools and frameworks into your projects.

What Makes This Book Different?

This book doesn't just teach you how to build APIs; it teaches you how to build **robust**, **scalable**, and **secure** APIs using **Python**. We focus on:

- **Real-World Examples**: Every chapter is filled with practical, real-world examples that demonstrate how the concepts apply in everyday development scenarios.
- **Hands-On Approach**: You'll learn by doing, with step-by-step instructions and code examples that you can follow along with and apply to your own projects.
- **Best Practices**: The book emphasizes best practices and provides guidance on structuring, testing, documenting, and securing your API, so you can confidently deploy it in production.

A Note on the Technologies Covered

- **Flask**: A lightweight and flexible micro-framework that is perfect for developers who prefer simplicity and control over their application.

- **Django**: A high-level framework that comes with a lot of built-in features and is ideal for building more complex and feature-rich APIs.
- **Celery**: For handling background tasks and improving API performance through asynchronous task processing.
- **Swagger/OpenAPI**: For automatically generating and presenting clean, interactive API documentation that makes it easier for developers to use your API.
- **Redis and Caching**: To help scale your API and manage heavy traffic by storing commonly used data in memory.

What You Can Expect After Reading This Book

By the end of this book, you will be equipped with a strong understanding of how to build, secure, and manage **RESTful APIs** using Python. You'll be able to create **Flask** and **Django** APIs from scratch, scale them to handle high traffic, and integrate them with databases and third-party services. You'll also learn how to consume external APIs and build clear, interactive documentation to help others use your API effectively.

This knowledge will set you on the path to becoming proficient in API development, a skill that is in high demand in today's tech industry. Whether you're working on internal services, building products for clients, or creating a public API for widespread use, the concepts in this book will help you build APIs that are reliable, efficient, and scalable.

Let's Get Started

If you're ready to build powerful APIs and enhance your development skills, let's dive into the world of Python-based **RESTful API** development. Grab your favorite text editor, fire up your Python environment, and let's start coding!

CHAPTER 1

INTRODUCTION TO RESTFUL APIS AND PYTHON

In this chapter, we will introduce the concept of RESTful APIs, explain their relevance in modern software development, and demonstrate how Python plays a vital role in creating robust web services. Whether you are new to web development or an experienced programmer, this chapter will lay the foundation for building and consuming APIs effectively using Python.

1.1 Overview of Web Services and APIs

Web services and APIs (Application Programming Interfaces) have become cornerstones of modern software systems, enabling communication and integration between different applications, platforms, and devices. But what exactly are they, and why do they matter?

- **What is a Web Service?** A **web service** is a system designed to support machine-to-machine interaction over a network, typically the internet. It allows applications to exchange data and services, regardless of the programming languages or platforms they are built on.

15

- **What is an API?** An **API (Application Programming Interface)** is a set of rules and protocols that allows software applications to communicate with each other. In simple terms, an API is a bridge that enables one system to interact with another by exposing certain functionalities and data. APIs can be used for a wide range of services like fetching data, updating records, or triggering actions in a remote system.

- **The Role of APIs in Modern Tech** APIs have revolutionized the way developers build software. They allow for:
    - **Modularity**: Separate parts of a system can evolve independently.
    - **Reusability**: Services can be reused across multiple applications.
    - **Integration**: APIs facilitate the seamless integration of third-party services such as payment gateways, social media platforms, and mapping services.
    - **Scalability**: APIs enable horizontal scaling by allowing multiple systems to work together.

Real-World Example: Consider an e-commerce platform that integrates payment processing via the **Stripe API**. By using Stripe's API, the platform can securely process payments without building a payment system from scratch, saving time and resources.

1.2 What is a RESTful API?

Now that we understand the role of APIs, let's dive into **RESTful APIs**, a popular design pattern for creating web services.

- **What is REST? REST (Representational State Transfer)** is an architectural style for designing networked applications. A RESTful API adheres to REST principles, offering simplicity and scalability. It focuses on stateless communication and uses standard HTTP methods for communication.
- **Principles of RESTful APIs** RESTful APIs follow a set of architectural principles to ensure they are simple, flexible, and scalable:
  - **Stateless**: Each request from a client to a server must contain all the necessary information for the server to understand the request. The server does not store any information about the client's state between requests.
  - **Client-Server Architecture**: The client (which could be a web browser or mobile app) interacts with the server, and the server handles business logic and data storage. The client and server are independent of each other, allowing for better separation of concerns.

17

- o **Uniform Interface**: A RESTful API uses consistent, standard operations such as HTTP methods (GET, POST, PUT, DELETE). This simplifies the interactions between the client and server.

- o **Resource-Based**: REST APIs are based on the concept of resources (like users, products, or orders). These resources are identified by URLs (Uniform Resource Locators), and the client can interact with them using HTTP methods.

- o **Stateless Communication**: Each interaction is independent of the previous one, ensuring scalability and simplicity.

- **How RESTful APIs Differ from Other API Architectures** While RESTful APIs are popular, there are other architectures to be aware of:

  - o **SOAP (Simple Object Access Protocol)**: SOAP is an older API standard that uses XML and focuses on strict standards and protocols. Unlike REST, SOAP is not as flexible or easy to use.

  - o **GraphQL**: GraphQL is a newer query language for APIs. It allows clients to request only the data they need, unlike REST, where clients fetch pre-defined sets of data.

Real-World Example: Consider a social media application's API. A RESTful API might have an endpoint like `GET` `/users/{id}`, which returns information about a specific user. A GraphQL API, on the other hand, might allow a client to request exactly which user information they need, like `query { user(id: 1) { name, email } }`.

1.3 Python's Role in Web Development

Python has gained tremendous popularity in web development, and its role in building APIs and web services is pivotal.

- **Why Python?** Python is known for its simplicity, readability, and flexibility, making it an ideal choice for web development. With frameworks like **Flask** and **Django**, Python offers powerful tools to quickly build APIs and web applications.
- **Python Frameworks for Building RESTful APIs**
  - **Flask**: Flask is a lightweight micro-framework that allows for rapid development of small to medium-sized applications. It's simple and gives developers full control over how their API is structured.
  - **Django**: Django is a more comprehensive, full-stack web framework that includes tools for database management, authentication, and routing. With the **Django Rest Framework**

(DRF), it is easy to build RESTful APIs with a lot of built-in features like authentication, pagination, and permissions.

Real-World Example: A company might use **Flask** for building a simple API that provides weather information, while **Django** could be used by an enterprise to build a complex, secure API for managing user data and payment transactions.

- **Benefits of Using Python for APIs**
  - **Ease of Learning**: Python's syntax is simple, making it easier for developers to pick up and start working on APIs without steep learning curves.
  - **Scalability**: Python frameworks like Flask and Django are highly scalable and can be used for small projects or large, complex web services.
  - **Community Support**: Python has a large and active community that provides tutorials, documentation, and third-party packages, making it easier to solve problems and learn new techniques.

Summary of Key Concepts

In this chapter, we've:

- Introduced web services and APIs, explaining their role in modern software systems.
- Discussed the key principles of RESTful APIs and how they differ from other architectures like SOAP and GraphQL.
- Explored Python's role in web development, highlighting how Flask and Django can help you build powerful and scalable APIs.

By the end of this chapter, you should have a solid understanding of what APIs are, why RESTful APIs are so widely used, and how Python plays a crucial role in developing them.

In the following chapters, we'll dive deeper into the practical aspects of building RESTful APIs with Python, including setting up your development environment, creating API endpoints, working with databases, and deploying your API to the cloud. Stay tuned!

CHAPTER 2

SETTING UP YOUR DEVELOPMENT ENVIRONMENT

Before you can start building and consuming APIs with Python, you need to set up your development environment. This chapter will walk you through installing Python, setting up a virtual environment, and introducing the tools and libraries you'll use to build RESTful APIs. Whether you're on **Windows**, **macOS**, or **Linux**, we'll make sure you're ready to go with the right tools.

2.1 Installing Python and Setting Up a Virtual Environment

To get started, you'll need Python installed on your machine. We'll walk through the installation process for different operating systems and then show you how to set up a **virtual environment** to manage your dependencies efficiently.

Installing Python

- **Windows**:
    1. Go to the official Python website and download the latest Python version.

2. Run the installer and make sure to check the box that says **"Add Python to PATH"**. This ensures that Python can be accessed from the command line.

3. Click "Install Now" and follow the installation instructions.

- **macOS**:

   1. macOS usually comes with Python pre-installed. You can check the version by running `python3 --version` in the terminal.

   2. If it's not installed or you need a specific version, you can use **Homebrew** to install it. Run the following commands:

```bash

brew update
brew install python
```

   3. Verify the installation with `python3 --version`.

- **Linux (Ubuntu/Debian-based)**:

   1. Python can be installed using the package manager. Open the terminal and type the following command:

```bash
```

```
sudo apt update
sudo apt install python3 python3-pip
```

2. Check the version by running `python3 --version`.

Setting Up a Virtual Environment

A **virtual environment** helps manage dependencies specific to a project, ensuring that libraries do not interfere with each other across different projects.

- **Creating a Virtual Environment**:
    1. Install **virtualenv** (if you don't have it already):

    bash

    ```
    pip install virtualenv
    ```

    2. Navigate to your project directory and create a new virtual environment:

    bash

    ```
    virtualenv venv
    ```

    This creates a directory called `venv` that holds all your project's dependencies.

- **Activating the Virtual Environment**:
  - **Windows**:

    ```bash
    venv\Scripts\activate
    ```

  - **macOS/Linux**:

    ```bash
    source venv/bin/activate
    ```

- When the virtual environment is active, your terminal prompt will change to indicate this. You can now install dependencies that are specific to your project.

2.2 Introduction to IDEs and Text Editors

Choosing the right Integrated Development Environment (IDE) or text editor is an important step for Python web development. Here's a list of the most popular choices for Python developers.

Popular Python IDEs and Text Editors

- **Visual Studio Code (VS Code)**:
  - A free, open-source editor with great support for Python. It features syntax highlighting, auto-

25

completion, debugging tools, and an integrated terminal.

- o To set it up, you'll need to install the **Python extension**:

    1. Open VS Code and go to the Extensions view (Ctrl+Shift+X).
    2. Search for **Python** and install the official extension.

- **PyCharm**:
    - o A powerful, feature-rich IDE specifically designed for Python. PyCharm offers a community edition for free, as well as a paid professional edition with more features like database support and remote development tools.
    - o You can download PyCharm from the official website.

- **Sublime Text**:
    - o A fast, lightweight text editor that supports Python with the right plugins. It's less heavy-duty than an IDE but still offers features like syntax highlighting and auto-completion.
    - o Install the **Anaconda** plugin for enhanced Python development features.

- **Atom**:
    - o Another free, open-source text editor. It's customizable and can be turned into a Python

development environment with the right packages, such as **ide-python**.

Choosing the Best Tool for You

- **Beginner-Friendly**: If you're just starting, **VS Code** is a great choice because of its simplicity, wide range of extensions, and a huge community.
- **Power Users**: If you need more advanced features like database integration, **PyCharm** is a great IDE.
- **Lightweight Option**: If you prefer minimal setups, **Sublime Text** or **Atom** may suit your style.

2.3 Installing Key Dependencies

Once you have Python installed and your development environment set up, the next step is to install the libraries and frameworks you'll need to build and consume RESTful APIs.

Introduction to `pip`

- **What is `pip`? `pip`** is the Python package installer that allows you to easily install and manage libraries. Most Python libraries are hosted on **PyPI (Python Package Index)**, and `pip` allows you to install them directly from the terminal.
- **Using `pip`**:

o To install a package:

```bash
```

```
pip install <package-name>
```

o To install a specific version:

```bash
```

```
pip          install        <package-
name>==<version>
```

o To list installed packages:

```bash
```

```
pip list
```

o To uninstall a package:

```bash
```

```
pip uninstall <package-name>
```

Installing Flask for API Development

Flask is a lightweight framework for building web applications and APIs. Here's how you can install it:

1. Make sure your virtual environment is activated.

2. Install Flask using `pip`:

```bash
```

```
pip install Flask
```

3. Once installed, you can verify the installation by running:

```bash
```

```
python -m flask --version
```

Installing Django for Advanced API Development

Django is a high-level Python web framework that's great for building larger applications. You can use **Django Rest Framework (DRF)** to build RESTful APIs.

1. To install Django, run:

```bash
```

```
pip install Django
```

2. To install Django Rest Framework, run:

```bash
```

```
pip install djangorestframework
```

Other Useful Libraries

Here are some additional libraries that might come in handy when building APIs:

- **Flask-RESTful**: Simplifies the creation of RESTful APIs with Flask.

  bash

  ```
  pip install Flask-RESTful
  ```

- **Requests**: A popular HTTP library for making requests to APIs.

  bash

  ```
  pip install requests
  ```

- **SQLAlchemy**: A powerful ORM for managing databases in Python.

  bash

  ```
  pip install SQLAlchemy
  ```

Summary of Key Concepts

In this chapter, you've learned how to:

- Install Python and set up a **virtual environment** for managing project-specific dependencies.
- Choose the right **IDE or text editor** based on your preferences and skill level.
- Use `pip` to install key dependencies, including **Flask** and **Django**, for building RESTful APIs.

By the end of this chapter, you should have a fully functional Python development environment ready to start building your RESTful APIs. In the next chapters, we'll start writing your first API endpoints using Flask and Django, allowing you to put your new setup to work!

CHAPTER 3

INTRODUCTION TO HTTP AND WEB REQUESTS

In this chapter, we will dive into the essential components of HTTP (HyperText Transfer Protocol), which is the foundation for RESTful APIs. Understanding HTTP methods, status codes, headers, and body is crucial for working with web services. We'll break down these concepts and show you how they play a role in real-world API interactions.

3.1 Understanding HTTP Methods (GET, POST, PUT, DELETE, etc.)

HTTP methods define the actions that can be performed on the resources exposed by an API. RESTful APIs rely on these methods to specify the kind of operation a client wants to perform on a resource.

Here's a breakdown of the most commonly used HTTP methods and real-world examples of how they are used in RESTful APIs:

GET - Retrieving Data

- **Purpose**: The GET method is used to retrieve data from the server. It is a read-only operation, meaning it does not modify any resources.
- **Real-World Example**: Imagine you are building an API for a blog. To retrieve a list of all blog posts, you would use a GET request.

```bash
GET /posts
```

This request would return all posts in a JSON format:

```json
[
  { "id": 1, "title": "My First Post",
"content": "This is my first blog post!" },
  { "id": 2, "title": "Another Post",
"content": "Here's some more content." }
]
```

POST - Creating Data

- **Purpose**: The POST method is used to submit data to the server to create a new resource. It is typically used to submit forms or create new records.

- **Real-World Example**: If a user submits a contact form on a website, you would send a POST request to create a new contact record.

```bash
POST /contacts
```

Request body (JSON):

```json
{   "name":   "John   Doe",   "email":
"john@example.com", "message": "Hello!" }
```

The server might respond with a status indicating that the contact was successfully created.

PUT - Updating Data

- **Purpose**: The PUT method is used to update an existing resource. Unlike POST, which creates new data, PUT modifies existing resources.
- **Real-World Example**: If a user wants to update their profile information, a PUT request would be sent to update that data.

```bash
```

```
PUT /users/123
```

Request body (JSON):

```
json
```

```json
{ "name": "John Doe", "email":
"newemail@example.com" }
```

DELETE - Removing Data

- **Purpose**: The DELETE method is used to delete a resource from the server.
- **Real-World Example**: If a user wants to delete their account, a DELETE request would be sent to remove their record.

```
bash
```

```
DELETE /users/123
```

PATCH - Partially Updating Data

- **Purpose**: The PATCH method is used to partially update a resource, modifying only the fields that need to be changed.
- **Real-World Example**: If you want to update just the email address of a user, you would send a PATCH request.

```
bash
```

35

```
PATCH /users/123
```

Request body (JSON):

```
json
```

```
{ "email": "newemail@example.com" }
```

OPTIONS - Checking Allowed Methods

- **Purpose**: The OPTIONS method is used to query the server about which HTTP methods are allowed on a particular resource. It's often used in pre-flight requests for CORS (Cross-Origin Resource Sharing) handling.
- **Real-World Example**: A browser might send an OPTIONS request before making a POST request to check whether the server allows it.

HEAD - Retrieving Headers

- **Purpose**: Similar to GET, but it only retrieves the headers of a resource, not the actual data.
- **Real-World Example**: This is often used for checking metadata, such as the last modified date, before deciding to download the full content.

3.2 What is a Status Code?

HTTP status codes are used to indicate the outcome of an HTTP request. They provide important feedback to the client about the status of the request. Here's an overview of the different classes of HTTP status codes and some common examples:

1xx - Informational Responses

- **100 Continue**: The request has been received, and the client can continue the request.
- **101 Switching Protocols**: The server is changing the protocol according to the client's request.

2xx - Successful Responses

- **200 OK**: The request was successful, and the server has returned the requested data.
  - o **Real-World Example**: A GET request for a list of blog posts returns a 200 status with the posts' data.
- **201 Created**: The request was successful, and a new resource was created (often used with POST).
  - o **Real-World Example**: When a new user is registered, a POST request returns a 201 status indicating the user has been created.

3xx - Redirection Responses

- **301 Moved Permanently**: The resource has been permanently moved to a new URL.
- **302 Found**: The resource has temporarily moved to a different URL.

4xx - Client Errors

- **400 Bad Request**: The request is malformed or missing required parameters.
  - **Real-World Example**: A POST request to create a new blog post with a missing title or invalid data might return a 400 status.
- **401 Unauthorized**: The client is not authenticated or the authentication failed.
  - **Real-World Example**: An API requires an API key or login credentials, and the request is missing this information.
- **403 Forbidden**: The client is authenticated but does not have permission to access the resource.
  - **Real-World Example**: A user tries to access an admin page they are not authorized to view.
- **404 Not Found**: The requested resource could not be found.

- o **Real-World Example**: A `GET` request for /posts/1234 returns a 404 status if the post with ID 1234 does not exist.
- **405 Method Not Allowed**: The HTTP method used is not allowed for the requested resource.
  - o **Real-World Example**: A `PUT` request to /posts when only `GET` and `POST` are allowed would return a 405 status.

5xx - Server Errors

- **500 Internal Server Error**: The server encountered an unexpected error while processing the request.
  - o **Real-World Example**: A bug in the backend code results in the server being unable to process the request.
- **502 Bad Gateway**: The server received an invalid response from an upstream server.
- **503 Service Unavailable**: The server is temporarily unable to handle the request due to maintenance or overloading.

3.3 HTTP Headers and Body

HTTP headers and the body are crucial for passing additional information between the client and the server. They allow clients and servers to communicate meta-information, handle authentication, and define the type of data being sent or expected.

Request Headers

Request headers provide metadata about the request. Some important ones include:

- **Content-Type**: Specifies the type of data being sent in the request body (e.g., `application/json`).
    - o **Real-World Example**: When sending JSON data in a `POST` request, you would include the header:

    ```bash
    bash
    ```

    ```
    Content-Type: application/json
    ```

- **Authorization**: Used to send credentials for authenticating the user.
    - o **Real-World Example**: An API key or a token is sent as part of the authorization header:

    ```bash
    bash
    ```

    ```
    Authorization: Bearer <your-token-here>
    ```

- **Accept**: Indicates what content types the client is willing to receive.

o **Real-World Example**: A client might request JSON responses:

```bash
```

```bash
Accept: application/json
```

Response Headers

Response headers provide metadata about the response from the server. Some key response headers are:

- **Content-Type**: Specifies the type of data being returned by the server (e.g., `application/json`).
  - o **Real-World Example**: A server might respond with JSON data:

```bash
```

```bash
Content-Type: application/json
```

- **Location**: Often used with `POST` or `PUT` requests to specify the location of the newly created resource.
  - o **Real-World Example**: After creating a new user, the server might return:

```bash
```

```bash
Location: /users/123
```

Request and Response Body

The **body** of an HTTP request or response contains the actual data being sent or received. It is used to transfer the resource itself.

- **Request Body**: Contains data that you are sending to the server, typically in JSON or form-encoded format.
  - **Real-World Example**: When creating a new blog post, the POST request body might look like this:

    ```json
    { "title": "New Post", "content": "This is a new blog post" }
    ```

- **Response Body**: Contains the data returned by the server in response to a request, usually in JSON format.
  - **Real-World Example**: When retrieving a list of blog posts, the response might be:

    ```json
    [
      { "id": 1, "title": "My First Post", "content": "Content of the first post" },
    ```

```
{ "id": 2, "title": "Another Post",
"content": "Content of another post"
}
]
```

Summary of Key Concepts

In this chapter, we've:

- Explored the main HTTP methods (GET, POST, PUT, DELETE, etc.) and how they are used in real-world RESTful APIs.
- Discussed the importance of HTTP status codes and provided examples of common codes such as 200, 404, and 500.
- Analyzed HTTP headers and body, focusing on how they carry metadata and data between the client and server.

With these core concepts in place, you are now equipped to understand how HTTP works under the hood of RESTful APIs. In the next chapters, we'll start applying these concepts by building actual APIs using Python.

CHAPTER 4

INTRODUCTION TO FLASK AND DJANGO FOR API DEVELOPMENT

In this chapter, we'll take an in-depth look at two of the most popular frameworks for building APIs with Python: **Flask** and **Django**. We'll compare them based on their strengths and use cases, and walk through setting up both frameworks to build your first API.

4.1 Overview of Flask and Django

Before diving into code, it's important to understand the fundamental differences between **Flask** and **Django** so you can choose the best one for your project needs.

Flask: The Lightweight Framework

- **Philosophy**: Flask is a minimalistic, lightweight web framework designed for flexibility and simplicity. It gives you the freedom to build your applications the way you want without much boilerplate code.

- **Use Cases**: Flask is ideal for small-to-medium-sized applications or microservices where you only need to implement basic API functionality and want to keep the project simple and customizable.
- **Pros**:
  - Lightweight and flexible.
  - Ideal for smaller projects or APIs.
  - Very minimal setup required.
  - Easy to learn for beginners.
- **Cons**:
  - Lacks built-in features for larger applications (e.g., authentication, database migrations).
  - Requires you to manually add third-party libraries for features you may need.

Django: The Full-Stack Framework

- **Philosophy**: Django is a full-stack, batteries-included web framework that comes with a lot of built-in tools and features for large applications. It's opinionated, meaning it enforces a certain way of doing things to keep your project organized and scalable.
- **Use Cases**: Django is better suited for building large, feature-rich applications or APIs where you need rapid development with lots of built-in features like authentication, user management, and ORM (Object-Relational Mapping).

45

- **Pros**:
    - Full-fledged framework with a lot of built-in functionality.
    - Great for large applications, complex projects, or when building CRUD-heavy APIs.
    - Built-in admin panel for database management.
    - Django Rest Framework (DRF) simplifies API development with advanced features like authentication and serialization.
- **Cons**:
    - Can be overkill for small projects.
    - Less flexibility compared to Flask.
    - Steeper learning curve due to its large set of features.

4.2 Setting Up Flask

Flask is an excellent choice if you want a lightweight, easy-to-learn framework for building APIs. Here, we'll set up a simple **Flask app** to demonstrate how easy it is to create an API with Flask.

Installing Flask

1. First, activate your virtual environment if it's not already active:

```bash
bash
```

```bash
source venv/bin/activate   # macOS/Linux
venv\Scripts\activate      # Windows
```

2. Then, install Flask:

```bash
bash
```

```bash
pip install Flask
```

Creating Your First Flask App

1. Create a new directory for your project, and inside that directory, create a Python file (e.g., app.py).
2. Now, let's write some code. Here's how you can create a simple **Flask API** with one endpoint (GET /hello) that returns a welcome message:

```python
python
```

```python
from flask import Flask, jsonify

app = Flask(__name__)

@app.route('/hello', methods=['GET'])
def hello_world():
    return          jsonify(message="Hello,
World!")
```

47

```
if __name__ == '__main__':
    app.run(debug=True)
```

3. **Explanation of the Code**:

   o `Flask(__name__)`: This creates a new Flask application instance.

   o `@app.route('/hello',`
   `methods=['GET'])`: This decorator defines a route for the API endpoint `/hello` that only accepts `GET` requests.

   o `jsonify()`: Flask provides a built-in function to return data as JSON. Here, we return a dictionary with a message.

   o `app.run(debug=True)`: This runs the app in debug mode, which helps during development by providing detailed error messages.

4. **Running the Flask App**:

   o To run the app, open your terminal, navigate to your project directory, and run:

   ```bash
   python app.py
   ```

   o Open your browser or use a tool like Postman to visit `http://127.0.0.1:5000/hello`, and you should see the following JSON response:

```
json

{
    "message": "Hello, World!"
}
```

4.3 Setting Up Django

Django is a bit more involved than Flask, but it offers more built-in functionality, making it a great choice for larger, more complex projects.

Installing Django

1. If you don't have Django installed, you can install it using `pip`:

   ```bash
   pip install Django
   ```

2. Then, install the **Django Rest Framework (DRF)**, which simplifies API development:

   ```bash
   pip install djangorestframework
   ```

Creating a New Django Project

1. Start a new Django project:

    bash

    ```bash
    django-admin startproject myproject
    cd myproject
    ```

2. Create a new Django app for your API:

    bash

    ```bash
    python manage.py startapp api
    ```

3. Now, let's create a simple API endpoint using **Django Rest Framework**.

Setting Up the API Endpoint

1. In the `api` app, create a file called `views.py` and add the following code:

    python

    ```python
    from rest_framework.views import APIView
    from rest_framework.response import Response
    from rest_framework import status
    ```

```
class HelloWorld(APIView):
    def get(self, request):
        return          Response({"message":
"Hello,                          World!"},
status=status.HTTP_200_OK)
```

2. This code defines a simple API view using DRF's `APIView` class. The `get` method responds to `GET` requests with a JSON response.

3. Now, link this view to a URL. In the `api` app, create a `urls.py` file and add the following code:

python

```
from django.urls import path
from .views import HelloWorld

urlpatterns = [
    path('hello/',   HelloWorld.as_view(),
name='hello-world'),
]
```

4. Finally, include these URLs in your main project's `urls.py` file (found in the `myproject` folder):

python

```
from django.contrib import admin
from django.urls import path, include
```

```
urlpatterns = [
    path('admin/', admin.site.urls),
    path('api/', include('api.urls')),
]
```

Running the Django App

1. Apply the migrations and run the server:

```bash
bash
```

```
python manage.py migrate
python manage.py runserver
```

2. Visit `http://127.0.0.1:8000/api/hello/` in your browser or Postman, and you should receive the following JSON response:

```json
json
```

```json
{
    "message": "Hello, World!"
}
```

Summary of Key Concepts

In this chapter, we:

- Explored the differences between **Flask** and **Django** for building APIs, understanding when to use each framework.
- Created a simple **Flask API** that demonstrates how easy it is to set up a lightweight API with minimal code.
- Set up a basic **Django API** using the **Django Rest Framework**, highlighting the more feature-rich approach Django provides for API development.

Both Flask and Django are powerful tools for building APIs, with Flask offering flexibility and simplicity for smaller projects, and Django providing a more structured, feature-rich environment for larger, more complex applications. In the upcoming chapters, we'll delve deeper into using these frameworks to create fully functional, production-ready RESTful APIs.

CHAPTER 5

BUILDING YOUR FIRST API WITH FLASK

In this chapter, we will guide you through building your first API using **Flask**. You will learn how to create simple API endpoints, handle **GET** requests, and process query parameters and request bodies. By the end of this chapter, you will have a good understanding of how Flask works in the context of building APIs and be ready to handle more complex requests.

5.1 Creating a Simple API Endpoint

The first step in building any API is defining the endpoints that will serve the data. In Flask, this is done using the `@app.route()` decorator to bind functions to specific routes (URLs).

Creating a Simple GET Endpoint

Let's start by creating a basic **GET** endpoint that returns a JSON response. This is a simple but important concept, as most RESTful APIs rely on the GET method to fetch data.

1. **Set Up Your Flask Project**: First, ensure that Flask is installed in your virtual environment:

bash

```
pip install Flask
```

2. **Create Your Flask App**: Create a new Python file (e.g., app.py) and add the following code to set up the Flask application:

python

```
from flask import Flask, jsonify

app = Flask(__name__)

# Define a simple GET endpoint
@app.route('/hello', methods=['GET'])
def hello():
    return         jsonify(message="Hello,
World!")

if __name__ == '__main__':
    app.run(debug=True)
```

   o **Explanation**:

      ▪ Flask(__name__): This initializes the Flask application.

55

- `@app.route('/hello', methods=['GET'])`: This creates a route at `/hello` that listens for GET requests.
- `jsonify(message="Hello, World!")`: This returns a JSON response with a key-value pair: `"message": "Hello, World!"`.
- `app.run(debug=True)`: This runs the application in debug mode, which is useful during development as it provides error logs and auto-reloads the server when changes are made.

3. **Run the Flask App**: Open your terminal, navigate to the directory where `app.py` is located, and run:

```bash
bash
```

```
python app.py
```

This starts the Flask development server. By default, it runs on `http://127.0.0.1:5000/`.

4. **Testing the Endpoint**: Open your web browser or use **Postman** to test the endpoint by visiting:

```bash
bash
```

```
http://127.0.0.1:5000/hello
```

You should receive a JSON response like this:

```json

{

    "message": "Hello, World!"

}
```

5.2 Request Handling in Flask

Flask makes it easy to handle different types of requests, including **query parameters**, **request bodies**, and **headers**. In this section, we will focus on handling **query parameters** and **request bodies**, which are commonly used in RESTful APIs.

Handling Query Parameters

Query parameters are typically included in the URL after a ? symbol and are often used for filtering, searching, or paginating data. They come in the format key=value, and multiple parameters are separated by an &.

For example:

```bash
```

```
http://127.0.0.1:5000/hello?name=John&age=30
```

To access query parameters in Flask, you can use the `request.args` object.

Here's how you can modify your previous Flask app to handle query parameters:

1. **Modify the `hello` endpoint to accept query parameters**:

    python

    ```python
    from flask import Flask, jsonify, request

    app = Flask(__name__)

    @app.route('/hello', methods=['GET'])
    def hello():
        # Access query parameters
        name = request.args.get('name',
    'World')  # Default to 'World' if 'name' is
    not provided
        age = request.args.get('age',
    'unknown')  # Default to 'unknown' if 'age'
    is not provided

        return jsonify(message=f"Hello,
    {name}!", age=age)
    ```

```
if __name__ == '__main__':
    app.run(debug=True)
```

o **Explanation**:

- `request.args.get('name', 'World')`: This fetches the `name` query parameter from the URL. If the `name` parameter is not provided, it defaults to "`World`".

- `request.args.get('age', 'unknown')`: This fetches the `age` parameter with a default value of "`unknown`" if not provided.

2. **Testing the Query Parameters**:

   o Open your browser or use Postman to make a `GET` request to the following URL:

```bash
```

```
http://127.0.0.1:5000/hello?name=John&age=30
```

You should receive the following JSON response:

```json
```

```
{
    "message": "Hello, John!",
    "age": "30"
}
```

o   If you don't provide any query parameters, the defaults will be used:

bash

```
http://127.0.0.1:5000/hello
```

The response would be:

json

```
{
    "message": "Hello, World!",
    "age": "unknown"
}
```

Handling Request Bodies (POST Method)

When working with **POST** or **PUT** requests, data is typically sent in the request body. You'll often deal with **JSON** data when building RESTful APIs.

Flask provides the `request.get_json()` method to parse the JSON data from the request body.

Let's modify the app to handle a POST request that accepts a JSON body.

1. **Modify the Flask app to handle POST requests**:

python

```python
from flask import Flask, jsonify, request

app = Flask(__name__)

@app.route('/greet', methods=['POST'])
def greet():
    # Get JSON data from the request body
    data = request.get_json()
    name = data.get('name', 'Guest')   # Default to 'Guest' if 'name' is not provided
    message = f"Hello, {name}!"

    return jsonify(message=message)

if __name__ == '__main__':
    app.run(debug=True)
```

- o **Explanation**:
    - request.get_json(): This method parses the incoming JSON data in the

61

request body and returns it as a Python dictionary.

- `data.get('name', 'Guest')`: This fetches the `name` from the JSON body. If the name is not provided, it defaults to `"Guest"`.

2. **Testing the POST Request**:
   - Open Postman or any API client and make a POST request to:

   ```bash
   http://127.0.0.1:5000/greet
   ```

   - Set the **Body** to **raw** and **JSON** in Postman and send the following JSON:

   ```json
   { "name": "Alice" }
   ```

   - You should receive the following JSON response:

   ```json
   {
     "message": "Hello, Alice!"
   }
   ```

o If you send the request without a name:

```json
```

```json
{}
```

You'll receive the default message:

```json
```

```json
{
    "message": "Hello, Guest!"
}
```

Summary of Key Concepts

In this chapter, we:

- Created a simple **GET** endpoint in Flask that returns a JSON response.
- Handled **query parameters** to customize the API response.
- Built a **POST** endpoint that processes request bodies in JSON format and returns a customized response based on the received data.

With this knowledge, you're now able to build basic Flask APIs that handle both query parameters and request bodies. In future chapters, we will dive deeper into more advanced topics like database integration, authentication, and error handling.

CHAPTER 6

BUILDING YOUR FIRST API WITH DJANGO

In this chapter, we will guide you through setting up your first API project with **Django** and **Django Rest Framework (DRF)**. Django provides a more structured approach to web development, while DRF makes it easy to build and manage RESTful APIs. By the end of this chapter, you'll have a simple API up and running using Django and DRF.

6.1 Setting Up a Django Project

Before we dive into building API endpoints, let's first set up a Django project. We'll guide you through the installation process and show you how to configure your project for API development.

Step 1: Install Django and Django Rest Framework

First, ensure that you have **Django** and **Django Rest Framework** installed in your virtual environment.

1. **Activate your virtual environment** (if it's not already activated):

```bash
```

```
source venv/bin/activate    # macOS/Linux
venv\Scripts\activate       # Windows
```

2. **Install Django**:

```bash
```

```
pip install Django
```

3. **Install Django Rest Framework (DRF)**:

```bash
```

```
pip install djangorestframework
```

Step 2: Create a Django Project

Once Django and DRF are installed, you can create a new Django project.

1. Run the following command to start a new Django project:

```bash
```

```
django-admin startproject myproject
cd myproject
```

2. Now, create a new Django app within your project:

```bash
bash
```

```bash
python manage.py startapp api
```

3. The `api` app is where we will define our API endpoints.

Step 3: Configure Django Settings

We need to tell Django about DRF by adding it to the **INSTALLED_APPS** in the `settings.py` file.

1. Open the `settings.py` file located in the `myproject` folder.

2. Add `'rest_framework'` and `'api'` to the `INSTALLED_APPS` list:

```python
python
```

```python
INSTALLED_APPS = [
    ...
    'rest_framework',  # Add this line
    'api',  # Add this line for the 'api'
app
]
```

3. You may also want to configure **CORS** (Cross-Origin Resource Sharing) if your API will be accessed from different domains. To do this, you can install **django-cors-headers**:

```bash
bash

pip install django-cors-headers
```

Then add it to your INSTALLED_APPS:

```python
python

INSTALLED_APPS = [
    ...
    'corsheaders',
]

MIDDLEWARE = [
    ...

'corsheaders.middleware.CorsMiddleware',
# Add this line
]

CORS_ORIGIN_ALLOW_ALL = True  # Allows all
origins, can be restricted later.
```

Step 4: Migrate the Database

Django comes with a built-in ORM (Object-Relational Mapping) system. To get the database ready, run the following migration commands:

1. Apply the initial migrations to set up the database schema:

```bash
bash
```

```bash
python manage.py migrate
```

2. Create a superuser to access the Django admin (optional, for managing models):

```bash
bash
```

```bash
python manage.py createsuperuser
```

Follow the prompts to create your superuser.

6.2 Creating API Endpoints with Django Rest Framework (DRF)

Now that the project is set up, let's create our first API endpoint using **Django Rest Framework**. DRF makes it easy to build RESTful APIs by providing tools to define views, serializers, and routers.

Step 1: Define a Model

Before creating an API, let's define a simple model for our app. For this example, we'll create a `Post` model that will represent blog posts.

1. Open the `models.py` file in the `api` app and add the following code:

```
python

from django.db import models

class Post(models.Model):
    title                                        =
models.CharField(max_length=100)
    content = models.TextField()
    created_at                                   =
models.DateTimeField(auto_now_add=True)

    def __str__(self):
        return self.title
```

2. Now, run the migration commands to create the database table for the `Post` model:

```bash
bash

python manage.py makemigrations
python manage.py migrate
```

Step 2: Create a Serializer

In Django Rest Framework, a **serializer** converts complex data types (like Django models) into JSON format and vice versa.

1. Create a new file called `serializers.py` inside the `api` app and define a serializer for the `Post` model:

```python
from rest_framework import serializers
from .models import Post

class
PostSerializer(serializers.ModelSerialize
r):
    class Meta:
        model = Post
        fields = ['id', 'title',
'content', 'created_at']
```

- o **Explanation**: The `PostSerializer` converts `Post` model instances into JSON format. The `fields` attribute specifies the model fields to be serialized.

Step 3: Create a View

Next, we need to create a **view** to handle incoming requests. DRF provides the `APIView` class to create custom views for handling different HTTP methods.

1. Open the `views.py` file in the `api` app and add the following code to create a simple `GET` and `POST` endpoint:

```python
python
```

71

```python
from rest_framework.views import APIView
from     rest_framework.response     import
Response
from rest_framework import status
from .models import Post
from .serializers import PostSerializer

class PostList(APIView):
    def get(self, request):
        posts = Post.objects.all()   # Get
all posts from the database
        serializer = PostSerializer(posts,
many=True)
        return Response(serializer.data)


    def post(self, request):
        serializer                         =
PostSerializer(data=request.data)
        if serializer.is_valid():
            serializer.save()   # Save the
new post to the database
            return
Response(serializer.data,
status=status.HTTP_201_CREATED)
        return Response(serializer.errors,
status=status.HTTP_400_BAD_REQUEST)
```

o **Explanation**:

- get(self, request): This method handles GET requests. It retrieves all Post objects, serializes them, and returns the data as JSON.
- post(self, request): This method handles POST requests. It deserializes the incoming data, saves a new Post to the database, and returns the serialized data.

Step 4: Create a URL Route

Now, we need to link the view to a URL route so that it can be accessed via the web.

1. Create a urls.py file in the api app and add the following code:

python

```python
from django.urls import path
from .views import PostList

urlpatterns = [
    path('posts/',      PostList.as_view(),
name='post-list'),
]
```

2. Next, include these URLs in the main project's `urls.py` file:

```python
from django.contrib import admin
from django.urls import path, include

urlpatterns = [
    path('admin/', admin.site.urls),
    path('api/', include('api.urls')),    #
Include the API URLs
]
```

Step 5: Test the API

Now that everything is set up, let's test the API.

1. Run the Django development server:

```bash
python manage.py runserver
```

2. Use **Postman** or **curl** to test the API:
   o **GET Request**: To fetch all posts:

   ```bash
   http://127.0.0.1:8000/api/posts/
   ```

- o **POST Request**: To create a new post:
  - Set the request method to POST.
  - URL:
    ```
    http://127.0.0.1:8000/api/pos
    ts/
    ```
  - Body (JSON):

    ```json
    {
       "title": "My First Post",
       "content":   "This    is    the
    content of the post."
    }
    ```

- o If successful, you will receive a response like:
- o json
- o
- o {
- o   "id": 1,
- o   "title": "My First Post",
- o   "content": "This is the content of
  the post.",
- o   "created_at":   "2025-04-
  07T12:34:56.789Z"
- o }

Summary of Key Concepts

In this chapter, we:

- Set up a **Django project** and **Django Rest Framework (DRF)** to start building an API.
- Created a simple `Post` model to represent blog posts in the database.
- Defined a **serializer** to convert model data into JSON and vice versa.
- Built a basic **API endpoint** for fetching and creating posts using DRF's `APIView`.
- Configured URL routing to map the endpoint to a URL path.

With this foundation in place, you're ready to build more complex APIs, handle authentication, and integrate your application with databases and other services. In future chapters, we will explore more advanced topics like error handling, authentication, and pagination.

CHAPTER 7

WORKING WITH JSON DATA

JSON (JavaScript Object Notation) is the most widely used format for transmitting data in web APIs. It's lightweight, easy to read and write, and language-independent, making it ideal for communication between servers and clients. In this chapter, we'll explore how JSON works, how to convert Python objects to JSON, and how to handle JSON data in Flask and Django APIs.

7.1 Understanding JSON

JSON is a text-based format that represents structured data as key-value pairs. It's often used to exchange data between a server and a client in RESTful APIs.

Basic Structure of JSON

JSON consists of two main data structures:

- **Objects**: Represented by key-value pairs, enclosed in curly braces { }.
- **Arrays**: Ordered collections of values, enclosed in square brackets [ ].

Here's a basic example of a JSON object and an array:

```json
json

{
  "id": 1,
  "name": "John Doe",
  "email": "john@example.com",
  "active": true,
  "roles": ["admin", "user"],
  "address": {
    "street": "123 Main St",
    "city": "Hometown",
    "postal_code": "12345"
  }
}
```

In this example:

- id, name, email, and active are key-value pairs.
- roles is an array containing two values: "admin" and "user".
- address is a nested object containing the keys street, city, and postal_code.

Real-World Example of JSON in APIs

Consider a **RESTful API** for managing users. When a client makes a GET request to fetch user details, the server responds with a JSON object containing the user's data:

json

```json
{
  "id": 123,
  "username": "johndoe",
  "email": "johndoe@example.com",
  "profile": {
    "age": 30,
    "location": "New York"
  }
}
```

When sending data, like in a **POST** request, the client would typically send JSON in the body of the request:

json

```json
{
  "username": "janedoe",
  "email": "janedoe@example.com",
  "password": "securepassword123"
}
```

7.2 Converting Python Objects to JSON

Python has built-in support for handling JSON through the `json` module, which provides functions to convert Python objects into JSON and vice versa. This process is called **serialization** (converting Python objects into JSON) and **deserialization** (converting JSON into Python objects).

Serialization: Python to JSON

To send Python data in a JSON format, you need to serialize it. The `json.dumps()` method converts Python objects like dictionaries, lists, and tuples into a JSON-formatted string.

Here's an example:

```python
import json

# Python dictionary
user_data = {
    "id": 123,
    "username": "johndoe",
    "email": "johndoe@example.com",
    "active": True
}

# Serialize the dictionary to a JSON string
```

```
json_data = json.dumps(user_data)
print(json_data)
```

Output:

json

```
{"id": 123, "username": "johndoe", "email":
"johndoe@example.com", "active": true}
```

- `json.dumps()` converts the Python dictionary into a JSON-formatted string.
- Note that in JSON, `True` becomes `true`, and `None` becomes `null`.

Indentation and Formatting

You can format the JSON output to make it more readable using the `indent` parameter:

python

```
json_data = json.dumps(user_data, indent=4)
print(json_data)
```

Output:

json

```
{
```

81

```
"id": 123,
"username": "johndoe",
"email": "johndoe@example.com",
"active": true
}
```

7.3 Handling JSON in API Requests and Responses

Now that you understand JSON and how to serialize Python objects into JSON, let's explore how to handle JSON data in Flask and Django APIs. Specifically, we'll look at how to **receive** JSON data from a client and **send** JSON data as a response from the server.

Handling JSON in Flask

Flask provides the `request` object, which has a method called `get_json()` to parse incoming JSON data from the request body. Similarly, Flask's `jsonify()` function is used to return JSON responses.

Receiving JSON in Flask (POST Request)

Here's how to handle JSON data sent by the client in a POST request:

1. **Define a POST Endpoint**: This example demonstrates how to receive JSON data from a client and return a response.

python

```python
from flask import Flask, request, jsonify

app = Flask(__name__)

@app.route('/create-user', methods=['POST'])
def create_user():
    # Get JSON data from the request body
    data = request.get_json()

    # Access specific fields from the JSON data
    username = data.get('username')
    email = data.get('email')

    # Create a response
    response = {
        "message": f"User {username} with email
{email} created successfully."
    }

    return jsonify(response)

if __name__ == '__main__':
    app.run(debug=True)
```

2. **Test the POST Request**: You can use Postman or `curl` to send a `POST` request to `http://127.0.0.1:5000/create-user` with the following JSON body:

json

```
{
  "username": "janedoe",
  "email": "janedoe@example.com"
}
```

3. **Response**:

json

```
{
  "message": "User janedoe with email janedoe@example.com created successfully."
}
```

- The `request.get_json()` method parses the incoming JSON data and converts it into a Python dictionary, which we can then use in our code.
- The `jsonify()` function is used to convert the Python dictionary into a JSON response.

Handling JSON in Django (DRF)

Django Rest Framework (DRF) provides built-in tools for handling JSON data seamlessly. The `request.data` attribute automatically handles incoming JSON requests and converts them into Python data.

Receiving JSON in Django (POST Request)

Let's define a simple `POST` endpoint to receive JSON data in Django.

1. **Define a View**: In the `views.py` file of your `api` app, add the following code to handle JSON data:

python

```python
from rest_framework.views import APIView
from rest_framework.response import Response
from rest_framework import status
from rest_framework.decorators import api_view

@api_view(['POST'])
def create_user(request):
    # Get JSON data from the request body
    username = request.data.get('username')
    email = request.data.get('email')

    # Create a response
```

85

```
response = {
    "message": f"User {username} with email
{email} created successfully."
}
```

```
return                         Response(response,
status=status.HTTP_201_CREATED)
```

2. **Define a URL Route**: In `urls.py`, map the `create_user` view to a URL:

python

```python
from django.urls import path
from .views import create_user

urlpatterns = [
    path('create-user/', create_user),
]
```

3. **Test the POST Request**: Send a POST request to `http://127.0.0.1:8000/api/create-user/` with the following JSON body:

json

```json
{
  "username": "janedoe",
  "email": "janedoe@example.com"
```

```
}
```

4. **Response**:

```json
json

{
  "message":    "User    janedoe    with    email
janedoe@example.com created successfully."
}
```

- In Django, the `request.data` object automatically parses the incoming JSON body into a Python dictionary, making it easy to access the data.
- The response is returned using the DRF's `Response` object, which automatically converts Python dictionaries into JSON.

Summary of Key Concepts

In this chapter, we:

- Learned about **JSON** and its basic structure, which is widely used for data exchange in APIs.
- Explored how to **serialize Python objects into JSON** using the `json.dumps()` method.

87

- Handled **JSON in API requests and responses** using **Flask** and **Django Rest Framework** (DRF), including receiving JSON data in a `POST` request and returning JSON responses.

Working with JSON is an essential skill for building APIs, and both Flask and Django Rest Framework provide simple and efficient ways to manage JSON data. In the next chapters, we will dive into more advanced topics such as authentication, error handling, and integrating databases into your APIs.

CHAPTER 8

HANDLING USER AUTHENTICATION

Authentication is a critical component in web development, especially when dealing with RESTful APIs that manage sensitive data. It ensures that only authorized users can access specific resources, and it plays a key role in securing applications. In this chapter, we'll explore why authentication is important in RESTful APIs and show how to implement two common authentication methods: **Basic Authentication** in Flask and **JWT Authentication** in Django Rest Framework (DRF).

8.1 Why Authentication is Important

Authentication is the process of verifying the identity of a user or system. In the context of RESTful APIs, it ensures that only legitimate users or services can access or modify resources. Here's why it's crucial:

1. **Securing Sensitive Data**: APIs often handle sensitive data such as user information, payment details, or personal preferences. Without authentication, unauthorized users could gain access to this data.

89

2. **Preventing Unauthorized Access**: Authentication prevents malicious users from performing unauthorized actions, such as modifying data, accessing restricted areas, or executing privileged operations.

3. **Enabling User Roles and Permissions**: Authentication is typically paired with authorization, where different users are assigned different roles (e.g., admin, user, guest). This allows APIs to implement granular access control.

4. **Maintaining Session Integrity**: Through authentication, users can maintain a session with the server, ensuring that they stay logged in across multiple requests and transactions.

Real-World Example: A RESTful API for an e-commerce platform may require users to log in before placing an order. Without authentication, anyone could place an order on behalf of another user, potentially causing issues like fraud or misuse.

8.2 Basic Authentication with Flask

Flask offers a straightforward way to implement basic authentication, a simple form of authentication where users provide a username and password.

What is Basic Authentication?

In **Basic Authentication**, the client sends the username and password with each request. These credentials are encoded in **Base64** and included in the `Authorization` header of the HTTP request.

Here's how we can implement basic authentication in a Flask app.

Step 1: Install Flask-HTTPAuth

To implement basic authentication in Flask, we can use the `Flask-HTTPAuth` extension.

1. Install `Flask-HTTPAuth`:

   bash

   ```
   pip install Flask-HTTPAuth
   ```

Step 2: Set Up Basic Authentication

Here's an example of implementing basic authentication in a Flask app:

1. **Create the Flask app** (`app.py`):

   python

   ```
   from flask import Flask, jsonify
   ```

```python
from flask_httpauth import HTTPBasicAuth

app = Flask(__name__)
auth = HTTPBasicAuth()

# Dummy user data
users = {
    "admin": "password123",
    "guest": "guestpassword"
}

# Function to verify the username and
password
@auth.verify_password
def verify_password(username, password):
    if username in users and
users[username] == password:
        return username
    return None

# Define a protected route
@app.route('/protected', methods=['GET'])
@auth.login_required
def protected():
    return jsonify(message="Welcome to the
protected route!")

if __name__ == '__main__':
    app.run(debug=True)
```

Explanation:

- `Flask-HTTPAuth`: This extension helps manage basic authentication in Flask. We use the `@auth.verify_password` decorator to define a function that checks if the provided username and password match the data stored in the `users` dictionary.
- `@auth.login_required`: This decorator ensures that the `protected()` route is accessible only to authenticated users.

Step 3: Running the Flask App

Run the Flask app by executing the following command:

bash

```
python app.py
```

Step 4: Testing Basic Authentication

To test the authentication, use a tool like **Postman** or **curl** to send a request to the `/protected` route.

- **In Postman**:
    1. Set the **HTTP method** to GET.
    2. Use the **Authorization** tab to select **Basic Auth** and enter `admin` as the username and `password123` as the password.

93

3. Send the request. You should receive a response:

json

```
{
    "message":    "Welcome    to    the
protected route!"
}
```

- **In curl**:

bash

```
curl         -u          admin:password123
http://127.0.0.1:5000/protected
```

If you provide the wrong credentials, Flask will return a **401 Unauthorized** status code.

8.3 JWT Authentication in Django Rest Framework

In modern web applications, **JWT (JSON Web Tokens)** are widely used for **stateless authentication**. Unlike Basic Authentication, JWT tokens are more secure and flexible. The server issues a token to the client after the user logs in, and the client includes the token in the header of subsequent requests.

What is JWT Authentication?

JWT is a compact, URL-safe token that is used for securely transmitting information between a client and server as a JSON object. JWT tokens typically consist of three parts:

- **Header**: Information about how the token is signed.
- **Payload**: Contains the claims (e.g., user information).
- **Signature**: A cryptographic signature used to verify that the token has not been tampered with.

Step 1: Install Django Rest Framework and djangorestframework-simplejwt

1. **Install DRF and JWT package**:

   bash

   ```
   pip        install        djangorestframework
   djangorestframework-simplejwt
   ```

2. **Update settings.py**: Add `rest_framework` and `rest_framework_simplejwt` to INSTALLED_APPS:

   python

   ```
   INSTALLED_APPS = [
        'rest_framework',
        'rest_framework_simplejwt',
   ```

```
# Other apps...
]
```

Step 2: Create JWT Views for Login and Authentication

Let's create views to handle user login and JWT token issuance.

1. **Define the `views.py` file**:

    python

    ```python
    from rest_framework_simplejwt.views import
    TokenObtainPairView, TokenRefreshView
    from rest_framework.permissions import
    IsAuthenticated
    from rest_framework.views import APIView
    from rest_framework.response import
    Response

    # Create JWT token view (Login)
    class
    MyTokenObtainPairView(TokenObtainPairView
    ):
        pass

    # Refresh token view
    class
    MyTokenRefreshView(TokenRefreshView):
        pass
    ```

```python
# Protected view that requires JWT token
class ProtectedView(APIView):
    permission_classes = [IsAuthenticated]

    def get(self, request):
        return Response({"message": "You are authenticated!"})
```

- `MyTokenObtainPairView` handles issuing the access and refresh tokens.
- `MyTokenRefreshView` handles token refresh requests.
- `ProtectedView` is a view that requires authentication via JWT token, and it only returns a response if the user is authenticated.

Step 3: Set Up URLs

1. **Update `urls.py`** to include the JWT token views:

python

```python
from django.urls import path
from .views import MyTokenObtainPairView,
MyTokenRefreshView, ProtectedView

urlpatterns = [
    path('api/token/',
MyTokenObtainPairView.as_view(),
name='token_obtain_pair'),
```

```
    path('api/token/refresh/',
MyTokenRefreshView.as_view(),
name='token_refresh'),
    path('protected/',
ProtectedView.as_view(),
name='protected'),
]
```

Step 4: Testing JWT Authentication

1. **Get the JWT Token**: Use Postman or curl to send a POST request to the /api/token/ endpoint with the user's credentials:

bash

```
curl         -X         POST         -d
"username=johndoe&password=securepassword
123" http://127.0.0.1:8000/api/token/
```

The server will respond with an access token and a refresh token:

json

```
{
  "access": "your-access-token",
  "refresh": "your-refresh-token"
}
```

2. **Access Protected View**: Now, use the access token to make a request to the /protected/ route:

```bash
curl -H "Authorization: Bearer your-
access-token"
http://127.0.0.1:8000/protected/
```

If the token is valid, you'll receive a response:

```json
{
    "message": "You are authenticated!"
}
```

Summary of Key Concepts

In this chapter, we:

- Explored the importance of **authentication** in RESTful APIs to secure data and prevent unauthorized access.
- Implemented **Basic Authentication** in **Flask** using Flask-HTTPAuth, which requires users to provide a username and password.
- Set up **JWT Authentication** in **Django Rest Framework (DRF)** using djangorestframework-

`simplejwt`, allowing clients to authenticate and authorize requests with JWT tokens.

Authentication is a fundamental part of API development, and with the knowledge of both Basic Authentication and JWT, you're well-equipped to secure your APIs. In the next chapters, we will explore further authentication mechanisms, error handling, and more advanced features for building production-ready APIs.

CHAPTER 9

ERROR HANDLING AND VALIDATIONS

Error handling and data validation are critical components of building robust and reliable APIs. They ensure that your API can gracefully handle unexpected situations and provide meaningful feedback to the client. In this chapter, we will explore **common API errors** and how to handle them, as well as how to **validate input data** in Flask and Django to ensure that only valid data is processed.

9.1 Common API Errors and How to Handle Them

Every API will inevitably encounter errors, and it's important to handle these errors properly to ensure a smooth user experience and reliable service. Common API errors typically fall into categories such as **client errors**, **server errors**, and **validation errors**.

1. Client Errors (4xx Status Codes)

These errors occur when the client sends an invalid request. The most common client errors include:

- **400 Bad Request**: This error occurs when the request is malformed or missing required parameters.
  - o **Example**: A POST request to create a new user is missing the username field.
  - o **How to Handle**: Return a clear message that indicates which fields are missing or invalid.
- **401 Unauthorized**: This error occurs when authentication is required, but the client has not provided valid credentials.
  - o **Example**: A client makes a request to access a restricted resource without providing a valid JWT token.
  - o **How to Handle**: Respond with a message explaining that authentication is required.
- **404 Not Found**: This error occurs when the client tries to access a resource that does not exist.
  - o **Example**: A client attempts to get a user by ID, but the user with that ID does not exist in the database.
  - o **How to Handle**: Return a 404 status code and explain that the requested resource could not be found.

2. Server Errors (5xx Status Codes)

These errors occur on the server side and indicate that something went wrong with processing the request. The most common server errors include:

- **500 Internal Server Error**: This error occurs when the server encounters an unexpected situation that prevents it from fulfilling the request.
    - **Example**: A database connection fails unexpectedly.
    - **How to Handle**: Log the error and return a generic message to the client, such as "An unexpected error occurred."
- **502 Bad Gateway**: This error occurs when the server receives an invalid response from an upstream server.
    - **Example**: The API relies on a third-party service, but that service is down or unreachable.
    - **How to Handle**: Respond with a 502 status code and inform the client that there was an issue with the external service.

3. Validation Errors

Validation errors occur when the data provided by the client does not meet the expected format or criteria. For example, when a user submits a registration form with an invalid email address.

- **Example**: A client tries to submit a form with an invalid email format or missing required fields.

  o **How to Handle**: Respond with `422 Unprocessable Entity` or a `400 Bad Request` and provide details about the specific validation errors.

Best Practices for Handling Errors

- **Provide clear error messages**: The error message should indicate exactly what went wrong and how the client can correct the issue.
- **Use appropriate status codes**: Return the correct HTTP status code for the type of error. For example, use `400` for client errors and `500` for server errors.
- **Log the errors**: Always log server errors to track issues and help with debugging.
- **Ensure consistency**: Use a consistent format for error responses across your API.

Here's a basic example of how to handle errors in Flask and Django.

9.2 Validating Input Data

Validating the data provided by the client is essential to ensure that only valid and safe data is processed. This can prevent issues such as invalid data being inserted into a database or causing the application to crash.

1. Validating Input Data in Flask

Flask doesn't have built-in validation like Django, but it's easy to handle input validation manually or with the help of libraries like **WTForms or Marshmallow**.

Example: Validating User Input with Flask

1. Install **WTForms** for form validation:

```bash
pip install Flask-WTF
```

2. Create a simple form to validate user data:

```python
from flask import Flask, request, jsonify
from wtforms import Form, StringField,
validators
```

```python
app = Flask(__name__)

class UserForm(Form):
    username   =   StringField('Username',
[validators.DataRequired(),
validators.Length(min=4, max=25)])
    email      =        StringField('Email',
[validators.DataRequired(),
validators.Email()])


@app.route('/register', methods=['POST'])
def register():
    form = UserForm(request.form)
    if form.validate():
        # Proceed with registration
        return         jsonify(message="User
registered successfully!")
    else:
        return
jsonify(errors=form.errors), 400


if __name__ == '__main__':
    app.run(debug=True)
```

- **Explanation**:
  - o The `UserForm` uses WTForms to define validation rules for `username` and `email`.
  - o `validate()` checks if the data meets the validation criteria.

106

o   If validation fails, it returns the error messages as JSON.

Test the Validation:

To test the validation, you can send a POST request with invalid data, such as a missing username or incorrect email.

---

2. Validating Input Data in Django

Django has built-in validation that works seamlessly with Django models and forms. When working with APIs, **Django Rest Framework (DRF)** provides a powerful validation mechanism using **serializers**.

Example: Validating User Input with Django Rest Framework (DRF)

1. Define a serializer to validate input data:

```python
from rest_framework import serializers

class
UserSerializer(serializers.Serializer):
    username                          =
serializers.CharField(max_length=100)
    email = serializers.EmailField()
```

```
def validate_username(self, value):
    if len(value) < 4:
        raise
serializers.ValidationError("Username must
be at least 4 characters long.")
    return value
```

2. Create a view to handle the registration endpoint:

```python
from rest_framework.views import APIView
from rest_framework.response import Response
from rest_framework import status
from .serializers import UserSerializer

class RegisterUser(APIView):
    def post(self, request):
        serializer =
UserSerializer(data=request.data)
        if serializer.is_valid():
            # Process registration
            return Response({"message":
"User registered successfully!"},
status=status.HTTP_201_CREATED)
        return Response(serializer.errors,
status=status.HTTP_400_BAD_REQUEST)
```

3. Add the URL routing:

```python
python

from django.urls import path
from .views import RegisterUser

urlpatterns = [
    path('register/',
RegisterUser.as_view()),
    ]
```

Test the Validation:

When sending a POST request to the /register/ endpoint with invalid data, such as an email without the "@" symbol, DRF will automatically validate the data and return the errors:

```json
json

{
  "email": ["Enter a valid email address."]
}
```

Summary of Key Concepts

In this chapter, we:

- Discussed **common API errors** and how to handle them using appropriate HTTP status codes, clear error messages, and consistent formatting.

- Explored **input validation** in both **Flask** (using WTForms) and **Django Rest Framework** (using serializers). Validation ensures that only valid and properly formatted data is processed by the server.

- Emphasized **best practices** for error handling and validation to ensure your APIs are reliable, secure, and user-friendly.

Handling errors and validating input data are essential for building resilient APIs that provide meaningful feedback to clients and maintain data integrity. In the next chapters, we will dive into more advanced topics like pagination, filtering, and authentication.

CHAPTER 10

UNDERSTANDING API VERSIONING

As your application grows and evolves, changes to its API may be necessary, such as adding new features, modifying data structures, or deprecating old endpoints. **API versioning** is essential to ensure backward compatibility, maintain a smooth user experience, and allow clients to continue using older versions of the API while migrating to newer ones.

In this chapter, we will explore why API versioning is important, and we'll discuss the most common methods for implementing versioning: **path-based**, **query parameter-based**, and **header-based versioning**.

10.1 Why API Versioning is Important

API versioning allows you to introduce changes to your API without breaking existing clients or applications that depend on the previous version of the API. Here are some reasons why API versioning is crucial:

1. Backward Compatibility

As your API evolves, older clients may still rely on previous versions. Without versioning, updates to the API could break existing clients, causing disruptions in service. Versioning helps ensure that clients using older versions continue to function properly even as new features are added.

Example: Suppose your API previously returned a user's full name as a single field (e.g., `name: "John Doe"`), but you now want to split it into `first_name` and `last_name`. Without versioning, existing clients would break, as they would expect the `name` field. With versioning, you can keep the old version intact while introducing the new field structure in the new version.

2. Progressive Enhancement

API versioning allows you to introduce new features and improvements without forcing all users to adopt them immediately. New clients can adopt the latest version with new features, while older clients can continue to use the existing version until they are ready to upgrade.

Example: Your API might introduce new endpoints or functionality, such as adding social login options or integrating a new payment gateway. Users who haven't migrated to the new version can continue using the old version, while those who are ready to upgrade can start using the new version.

3. Clear Communication of Changes

Versioning helps communicate changes to consumers of your API in a clear and structured way. It provides a way to track and document changes made to the API and ensures that users know which version they are working with.

Example: If a client encounters an issue with an API, they can refer to the version number to ensure they are working with the correct set of features or functionality.

4. Security

Sometimes older versions of an API may contain vulnerabilities that have been fixed in newer versions. By introducing versioning, you can ensure that security patches are applied to newer versions, while allowing clients to continue using the older versions temporarily.

10.2 Methods for API Versioning

There are several common approaches to implementing versioning in RESTful APIs. Each method has its pros and cons, and the choice largely depends on your use case, the scale of your application, and the client requirements.

1. Path-Based Versioning

Path-based versioning is the most widely used method for API versioning. The version number is included directly in the URL path, making it easy for both the server and client to determine which version of the API they are interacting with.

Example:

bash

```
GET /api/v1/users/123
GET /api/v2/users/123
```

- **Advantages**:
  - Easy to implement and understand.
  - Makes it clear which version of the API is being used in the URL.
  - It's simple to manage different versions of the API independently.
- **Disadvantages**:
  - URL structure becomes longer as versions increase.
  - Potential for confusion if you don't properly document versioning rules.

Real-World Example:

GitHub's API uses path-based versioning. For instance:

- `GET /v1/users`: Access the v1 of the users API.
- `GET /v2/users`: Access the v2 of the users API.

This method works well when there are significant differences between API versions.

Implementation in Flask:

python

```
from flask import Flask, jsonify

app = Flask(__name__)

@app.route('/api/v1/users/<int:user_id>',
methods=['GET'])
def get_user_v1(user_id):
    # Logic for v1
    return jsonify(message=f"User {user_id} from
v1")

@app.route('/api/v2/users/<int:user_id>',
methods=['GET'])
def get_user_v2(user_id):
    # Logic for v2 (new features or changes)
```

```
    return jsonify(message=f"User {user_id} from
v2")

if __name__ == '__main__':
    app.run(debug=True)
```

2. Query Parameter-Based Versioning

Query parameter-based versioning places the version number as a query parameter in the URL. This method is less intrusive than path-based versioning and allows clients to easily change versions without modifying the URL path.

Example: /

bash

```
GET /api/users?version=1
GET /api/users?version=2
```

- **Advantages**:
  - o Simple to implement.
  - o Keeps the URL clean and can be added dynamically.
  - o Allows for easy version switching via query parameters.
- **Disadvantages**:
  - o It may be less intuitive, especially when APIs have a large number of versions.

116

- o It can lead to confusion if not documented properly.
- o It's easy to forget to include the version parameter in the request.

Real-World Example:

Some APIs, like **Slack**, use query parameters to manage versioning, although this approach is less common compared to path-based versioning.

Implementation in Flask:

python

```python
from flask import Flask, request, jsonify

app = Flask(__name__)

@app.route('/api/users', methods=['GET'])
def get_users():
    version = request.args.get('version', '1')  #
Default to version 1
    if version == '1':
        return jsonify(message="Users from v1")
    elif version == '2':
        return jsonify(message="Users from v2")
    else:
        return     jsonify(message="Version     not
supported"), 400
```

117

```
if __name__ == '__main__':
    app.run(debug=True)
```

3. Header-Based Versioning

Header-based versioning involves sending the version information in the HTTP request header rather than in the URL or query parameters. This method is less intrusive and keeps the URL clean, but requires clients to be aware of how to set custom headers.

Example:

bash

```
GET /api/users
Header: X-API-Version: 1
```

- **Advantages**:
  - Clean URLs and no need to modify the API path.
  - More flexible, especially when you have multiple versions but want to keep the URL consistent.
  - Allows clients to send versioning information without changing the structure of the URL.
- **Disadvantages**:
  - Requires clients to set custom headers, which may add complexity.
  - Not as widely adopted as path-based versioning.

118

o May not be ideal for APIs exposed to the public, as users may not always know how to set custom headers.

Real-World Example:

GitHub also supports header-based versioning. Their API requires users to send the version as a custom header (Accept header) in the request, such as:

bash

```
Accept: application/vnd.github.v3+json
```

Implementation in Flask:

python

```
from flask import Flask, request, jsonify

app = Flask(__name__)

@app.route('/api/users', methods=['GET'])
def get_users():
    version = request.headers.get('X-API-Version', '1')  # Default to version 1
    if version == '1':
        return jsonify(message="Users from v1")
    elif version == '2':
        return jsonify(message="Users from v2")
    else:
```

```
        return    jsonify(message="Version    not
supported"), 400

if __name__ == '__main__':
    app.run(debug=True)
```

Summary of Key Concepts

In this chapter, we've:

- Discussed the importance of **API versioning**, ensuring backward compatibility and smooth user experiences as APIs evolve.
- Explored the three main methods of API versioning: **path-based**, **query parameter-based**, and **header-based** versioning.
  - o **Path-based versioning** is the most common method, where the version is included in the URL path.
  - o **Query parameter-based versioning** places the version in the URL as a query parameter.
  - o **Header-based versioning** uses custom headers to specify the version, keeping URLs clean.

Each versioning method has its pros and cons, and the choice of method will depend on your application's needs, scalability, and the way your users interact with the API. Understanding API versioning is essential for maintaining a reliable, flexible, and scalable API over time.

CHAPTER 11

CONNECTING TO A DATABASE

In this chapter, we'll explore how to connect a RESTful API to a database, an essential step in building dynamic applications that require persistent data storage. We'll discuss the differences between **relational** and **NoSQL** databases, and then walk through examples of integrating a lightweight **SQLite** database with Flask and a more robust **PostgreSQL** database with Django.

11.1 Relational vs NoSQL Databases

When building APIs that interact with a database, it's important to choose the right type of database. **Relational** and **NoSQL** databases are the two most common types, each with its own strengths and use cases.

Relational Databases (RDBMS)

- **Examples**: PostgreSQL, MySQL, SQLite
- **Structure**: Data is stored in tables with rows and columns, and relationships are established between tables using foreign keys.
- **Use Cases**: Best for structured data, where relationships between entities are important (e.g., a customer with

122

orders or users with posts). Ideal for scenarios where you need complex queries, data integrity, and consistency.

- **Strengths**:
    - o Supports **ACID** (Atomicity, Consistency, Isolation, Durability) properties for reliable transactions.
    - o Excellent for applications that require structured data and complex querying.
    - o Widely supported and standardized (SQL).

NoSQL Databases

- **Examples**: MongoDB, CouchDB, Cassandra, Redis
- **Structure**: Data is stored in an unstructured or semi-structured way, using documents, key-value pairs, graphs, or wide-column stores. NoSQL databases are schema-less.
- **Use Cases**: Ideal for applications with large amounts of unstructured data, fast read/write operations, or scalability needs (e.g., social media platforms, IoT systems).
- **Strengths**:
    - o High scalability and flexibility in handling large, unstructured data.
    - o Schema flexibility allows for easy changes in data models.
    - o Optimized for performance and speed.

Real-World Example: If you're building an e-commerce app with customer orders and product catalogs, a **relational database** (e.g., **PostgreSQL**) would be a good fit because of the relationships between orders, products, and customers. However, if you're building a social media platform where users frequently post unstructured data (images, comments), a **NoSQL database** (e.g., **MongoDB**) would be more appropriate.

Choosing the Right Database for Your API Needs

- **Use a relational database** when your data is structured and requires complex queries or relationships (e.g., user data, financial records).
- **Use a NoSQL database** when scalability and flexibility in data modeling are key, or when your data is unstructured or semi-structured (e.g., social media feeds, logs, session data).

11.2 Using SQLite with Flask

SQLite is a lightweight, file-based relational database that is a great choice for small applications, prototyping, or applications where the database doesn't need to scale too much.

Setting Up SQLite with Flask

1. **Install SQLite**: Flask comes with built-in support for SQLite. To use SQLite, you'll need the `Flask-SQLAlchemy` extension, which simplifies working with databases in Flask.

   Install the necessary dependencies:

   ```bash
   pip install Flask-SQLAlchemy
   ```

2. **Create a Flask Application and Configure SQLite**: Below is an example of how to set up an SQLite database with Flask using **SQLAlchemy** for ORM (Object-Relational Mapping).

   ```python
   from flask import Flask, jsonify, request
   from flask_sqlalchemy import SQLAlchemy

   app = Flask(__name__)
   app.config['SQLALCHEMY_DATABASE_URI']    =
   'sqlite:///app.db'    # SQLite file-based
   database
   app.config['SQLALCHEMY_TRACK_MODIFICATION
   S'] = False
   ```

```python
db = SQLAlchemy(app)

# Define a User model
class User(db.Model):
    id          =          db.Column(db.Integer,
primary_key=True)
    username  =  db.Column(db.String(100),
nullable=False, unique=True)
    email     =    db.Column(db.String(100),
nullable=False, unique=True)

    def __repr__(self):
        return f'<User {self.username}>'

# Create the database tables
with app.app_context():
    db.create_all()

# Route to create a new user
@app.route('/users', methods=['POST'])
def create_user():
    data = request.get_json()
    new_user                                =
User(username=data['username'],
email=data['email'])
    db.session.add(new_user)
    db.session.commit()
```

```
        return  jsonify(message="User  created
successfully"), 201

# Route to fetch all users
@app.route('/users', methods=['GET'])
def get_users():
    users = User.query.all()
        return    jsonify([{'id':    user.id,
'username':    user.username,    'email':
user.email} for user in users])

if __name__ == '__main__':
    app.run(debug=True)
```

Explanation:

- SQLAlchemy is used to handle database interactions. The User model defines the structure of the users table.
- The SQLite database file (app.db) is created automatically when the app starts.
- **Creating the Database**: db.create_all() creates the database tables based on the defined models.

Step 3: Testing the Flask App with SQLite:

- Start the Flask application by running:

```
bash
```

```
python app.py
```

127

- You can now test the /users endpoint:
  - **POST** a new user:

```json
json

{
  "username": "john_doe",
  "email": "john@example.com"
}
```

  - **GET** all users:

```bash
bash

http://127.0.0.1:5000/users
```

11.3 Using PostgreSQL with Django

PostgreSQL is a powerful, open-source relational database that works well for larger, production-ready applications due to its scalability, support for advanced features (e.g., full-text search, JSONB), and strong community support.

Setting Up PostgreSQL with Django

1. **Install PostgreSQL and Psycopg2**: PostgreSQL requires the psycopg2 library to connect to the database. Install it using pip:

```bash
bash

pip install psycopg2
```

2. **Configure PostgreSQL Database in Django**: In Django, the database configuration is done in the `settings.py` file.

Here's how you can configure PostgreSQL:

```python
python

DATABASES = {
    'default': {
        'ENGINE':
'django.db.backends.postgresql',
        'NAME': 'mydatabase',    # Replace
with your database name
        'USER': 'myuser',        # Replace
with your database user
        'PASSWORD': 'mypassword',      #
Replace with your password
        'HOST': 'localhost',
        'PORT': '5432',        #  Default
PostgreSQL port
    }
}
```

129

3. **Create a Django Model**: Let's define a simple `User` model for PostgreSQL in `models.py`:

```python
python
```

```python
from django.db import models

class User(models.Model):
    username                          =
models.CharField(max_length=100,
unique=True)
    email = models.EmailField(unique=True)

    def __str__(self):
        return self.username
```

4. **Run Migrations**: Django uses migrations to apply changes to the database schema. Run the following commands to create the database tables based on the models:

```bash
bash
```

```bash
python manage.py makemigrations
python manage.py migrate
```

5. **Create Views and URLs**: Now, let's create a simple API endpoint to fetch users from PostgreSQL using **Django Rest Framework (DRF)**.

o   Install **DRF** if you haven't already:

```bash
pip install djangorestframework
```

o   Create a serializer in `serializers.py`:

```python
from        rest_framework       import
serializers
from .models import User

class
UserSerializer(serializers.ModelSer
ializer):
    class Meta:
        model = User
        fields = ['id', 'username',
'email']
```

o   Define a view in `views.py`:

```python
from    rest_framework.views   import
APIView
from  rest_framework.response  import
Response
```

131

```python
from .models import User
from .serializers import UserSerializer


class UserList(APIView):
    def get(self, request):
        users = User.objects.all()
        serializer = UserSerializer(users, many=True)
        return Response(serializer.data)
```

o Configure the URL route in `urls.py`:

```python
python
```

```python
from django.urls import path
from .views import UserList

urlpatterns = [
    path('users/', UserList.as_view(), name='user-list'),
]
```

Step 3: Testing the Django API with PostgreSQL:

- Start the Django development server:

```bash
bash
```

```
python manage.py runserver
```

- You can now test the API by navigating to http://127.0.0.1:8000/users/ to see the list of users fetched from PostgreSQL.

Summary of Key Concepts

In this chapter, we:

- Discussed the differences between **relational databases** (e.g., PostgreSQL, SQLite) and **NoSQL databases** and provided guidance on choosing the right database for your API needs.
- Walked through integrating an **SQLite** database with Flask for small applications or prototyping, showing how to create a simple user model and handle requests.
- Explained how to set up **PostgreSQL** with **Django** for larger, production-ready applications, and demonstrated how to create a model, apply migrations, and build a simple API using **Django Rest Framework (DRF)**.

Database integration is a crucial part of API development, and understanding how to connect and interact with different databases will enable you to build powerful, scalable, and dynamic APIs. In the next chapters, we will explore more advanced topics, such as database relationships, handling migrations, and optimizing performance.

CHAPTER 12

WORKING WITH EXTERNAL APIS

Integrating external APIs into your application can significantly enhance its functionality, whether you're pulling in third-party data, processing payments, or interacting with popular platforms like Twitter or Google Maps. In this chapter, we will focus on how to consume third-party APIs, handle API authentication, and manage errors gracefully when making API requests.

12.1 Consuming Third-Party APIs

Consuming third-party APIs means that your application will send requests to other services, retrieve data, and process it for your needs. Here are a few **real-world examples** of how external APIs are commonly used:

Example 1: Integrating Twitter API

The **Twitter API** allows you to interact with Twitter's platform, retrieve tweets, post updates, or even search for hashtags. If you're building a service that pulls tweets about a certain topic, you would use the Twitter API.

- **How to Use**: Twitter's API requires you to authenticate using **OAuth**, which is a secure authentication method that grants your application access to a user's account without sharing passwords.
- **Request**: To retrieve tweets from a certain hashtag, you might use an endpoint like:

```bash
GET
https://api.twitter.com/2/tweets/search/r
ecent?query=%23flask
```

Example 2: Integrating Stripe API for Payments

Stripe is a popular service for processing online payments. If you're building an e-commerce platform, Stripe would be a great API to integrate for handling payment transactions.

- **How to Use**: Stripe offers a well-documented API to handle payments, including creating charges, refunding payments, and handling subscriptions.
- **Request**: To create a payment charge, you would send a POST request to the Stripe API:

```bash
POST https://api.stripe.com/v1/charges
```

With the following body data (in JSON format):

```json
json

{
  "amount": 5000,
  "currency": "usd",
  "source": "tok_visa",
  "description": "Charge for product"
}
```

Example 3: Integrating Google Maps API

The **Google Maps API** allows your application to retrieve data about geographic locations, display maps, get directions, and much more.

- **How to Use**: You can use the API to display maps, search for locations, or even get directions.
- **Request**: To get the latitude and longitude of a specific location, you can use:

```bash
bash

GET
https://maps.googleapis.com/maps/api/geoc
ode/json?address=New+York&key=YOUR_API_KE
Y
```

Making API Requests in Python

To interact with third-party APIs, Python provides the `requests`
library, which is simple and powerful for sending HTTP requests.

Here's an example of consuming an external API (e.g., fetching
weather data):

```python
import requests

def get_weather(city):
    api_key = "your_api_key"
    base_url =
f"http://api.openweathermap.org/data/2.5/weathe
r?q={city}&appid={api_key}"
    response = requests.get(base_url)
    data = response.json()

    if response.status_code == 200:
        return data
    else:
        return {"error": "City not found or API
error"}

weather = get_weather("London")
print(weather)
```

In this example:

- The `requests.get()` function sends a GET request to the weather API.
- The response is parsed as JSON using `response.json()`, and the relevant weather data is extracted.

12.2 API Authentication

When consuming third-party APIs, authentication is often required. There are several ways to authenticate API requests, including **API keys** and **OAuth2**.

1. API Key Authentication

Many APIs require an API key, which is a unique identifier used to authenticate requests. This key is typically passed in the header or query parameters of the request.

Example: Sending an API Key in Headers

python

```python
import requests

def get_weather(city):
    api_key = "your_api_key"
```

```python
    headers = {
        "Authorization": f"Bearer {api_key}"
    }
    base_url                                =
f"http://api.openweathermap.org/data/2.5/weathe
r?q={city}"
    response        =        requests.get(base_url,
headers=headers)
    data = response.json()
    return data

weather = get_weather("London")
print(weather)
```

- **Explanation**: The `Authorization` header is used to send the API key along with the request. Some APIs might require the key as a query parameter instead of in the header.

2. OAuth2 Authentication

OAuth2 is a more secure and flexible authentication method used by APIs like Google, Twitter, and Facebook. It allows your app to access user data without exposing their password.

Steps for OAuth2 Authentication:

- **Step 1**: The user is redirected to the OAuth provider's login page.

- **Step 2**: After the user logs in, the provider redirects them back to your app with an **authorization code**.
- **Step 3**: Your app exchanges the authorization code for an **access token**, which can be used to make authenticated API requests.

Example: OAuth2 with Requests-OAuthlib

To authenticate with an OAuth2 service, you can use the `requests-oauthlib` library. Here's an example using GitHub's OAuth2:

1. **Install requests-oauthlib**:

   bash

   ```
   pip install requests-oauthlib
   ```

2. **OAuth2 Authentication Flow**:

   python

   ```
   from        requests_oauthlib        import
   OAuth2Session
   from requests.auth import HTTPBasicAuth

   client_id = 'your_client_id'
   client_secret = 'your_client_secret'
   redirect_uri = 'http://localhost/callback'
   ```

```python
authorization_base_url                  =
'https://github.com/login/oauth/authorize
'
token_url                               =
'https://github.com/login/oauth/access_to
ken'

# Create an OAuth2 session
oauth        =        OAuth2Session(client_id,
redirect_uri=redirect_uri)

# Get authorization URL
authorization_url,          state        =
oauth.authorization_url(authorization_bas
e_url)
print(f'Please  go  to  {authorization_url}
and authorize access.')

# After the user authorizes, they will be
redirected to the redirect_uri
#   You   will   need   to   capture   the
authorization response URL
redirect_response = input('Paste the full
redirect URL here: ')

# Fetch the access token using the response
URL
oauth.fetch_token(token_url,
authorization_response=redirect_response,
```

```
client_secret=client_secret,
auth=HTTPBasicAuth(client_id,
client_secret))


# Now you can make API calls on behalf of
the user
response                              =
oauth.get('https://api.github.com/user')
print(response.json())
```

- **Explanation**:
  - o The OAuth2Session object handles the OAuth2 flow.
  - o The user is redirected to GitHub's authorization page to grant access.
  - o The app exchanges the authorization code for an access token, which is used to make API requests on behalf of the user.

12.3 Error Handling When Consuming APIs

When consuming third-party APIs, things can go wrong. The API might be down, the request might fail due to network issues, or the data could be invalid. It's important to handle these errors gracefully to prevent your application from crashing and to provide meaningful feedback to users.

Handling HTTP Errors

When making API requests, it's important to check the status code of the response and handle different scenarios accordingly.

Example: Handling HTTP Errors with `requests`:

```python
python

import requests

def get_weather(city):
    api_key = "your_api_key"
    base_url                              =
f"http://api.openweathermap.org/data/2.5/weathe
r?q={city}&appid={api_key}"
    try:
        response = requests.get(base_url)
        response.raise_for_status()   # Raise an
exception for 4xx/5xx errors
        data = response.json()

        if response.status_code == 200:
            return data
        else:
            return {"error": "Failed to retrieve
data"}

    except    requests.exceptions.HTTPError    as
http_err:
```

```
    return {"error": f"HTTP error occurred:
{http_err}"}
    except requests.exceptions.RequestException
as req_err:
        return {"error": f"Error occurred:
{req_err}"}

weather = get_weather("London")
print(weather)
```

- **Explanation**:
    - ○ raise_for_status() raises an exception if the status code indicates an error (e.g., 400 or 500).
    - ○ Specific error messages are returned based on the type of error, such as HTTP errors or general request issues.

Rate Limiting and Retries

Some APIs have rate limits, meaning they can only handle a certain number of requests in a given time frame. If you exceed the limit, the API will respond with an error, usually 429 Too Many Requests.

Example: Handling Rate Limits and Retries:

python

```python
import time
import requests


def get_data_with_retries(url, max_retries=3):
    retries = 0
    while retries < max_retries:
        response = requests.get(url)
        if response.status_code == 429:
            # If rate-limited, wait for a while
before retrying
            print("Rate      limit      exceeded.
Retrying...")
            time.sleep(2)    # Wait  2  seconds
before retrying
            retries += 1
        else:
            return response.json()


    return {"error": "Max retries reached. Could
not fetch data."}

data                                             =
get_data_with_retries("http://example.com/api")
print(data)
```

- **Explanation**:
    - o This code retries the request if it encounters a 429 `Too Many Requests` error, with a delay between retries.

o After a specified number of retries, it returns an error message if the request still fails.

Summary of Key Concepts

In this chapter, we:

- Explored **consuming third-party APIs**, with real-world examples like integrating Twitter, Stripe, and Google Maps APIs into your application.
- Covered **API authentication**, including how to handle **API keys** and **OAuth2** for secure access to third-party services.
- Discussed **error handling** strategies for working with external APIs, such as handling HTTP errors, dealing with rate limits, and implementing retries for failed requests.

Integrating external APIs can greatly enhance your application's capabilities, but it's crucial to handle authentication, errors, and rate limits properly to ensure a smooth and secure experience for your users. In the next chapters, we'll dive into more advanced topics like pagination, filtering, and security.

147

CHAPTER 13

API TESTING AND DEBUGGING

Testing and debugging are crucial steps in building robust and reliable APIs. **Unit testing** ensures that individual components of your API are working as expected, while **debugging** tools help you identify and fix issues in your code. In this chapter, we'll walk through **unit testing** in **Flask** and **Django Rest Framework (DRF)**, and discuss useful **debugging techniques** for both frameworks.

13.1 Unit Testing with Flask

Flask is a lightweight web framework, and testing its APIs is made simple using **pytest** and Flask's built-in test client. Unit tests help you verify that your API endpoints and their corresponding logic are functioning as expected.

Setting Up Testing with Flask

1. **Install pytest**: First, install **pytest** and **pytest-flask** to enable testing with Flask.

   bash

```
pip install pytest pytest-flask
```

2. **Create a Test Configuration**: Create a `test_app.py` file for testing your Flask app.

3. **Write Unit Tests for API Endpoints**: Flask's **test client** allows you to simulate HTTP requests to your app and capture the response. Here's an example of unit tests for a simple POST and GET API.

Example Flask App (`app.py`):

```python
python

from flask import Flask, jsonify, request
app = Flask(__name__)

users = []

@app.route('/users', methods=['GET'])
def get_users():
    return jsonify(users)

@app.route('/users', methods=['POST'])
def create_user():
    data = request.get_json()
    users.append(data)
    return jsonify(message="User created
successfully"), 201
```

149

```
if __name__ == '__main__':
    app.run(debug=True)
```

Writing Unit Tests (test_app.py):

python

```
import pytest
from app import app

@pytest.fixture
def client():
    with app.test_client() as client:
        yield client

def test_create_user(client):
    response = client.post('/users',
json={'username': 'john', 'email':
'john@example.com'})
    assert response.status_code == 201
    assert response.json['message'] ==
"User created successfully"

def test_get_users(client):
    client.post('/users',
json={'username': 'john', 'email':
'john@example.com'})
    response = client.get('/users')
    assert response.status_code == 200
    assert len(response.json) == 1
```

```
assert response.json[0]['username'] ==
'john'
```

- o `client` is a **pytest fixture** that sets up Flask's test client.
- o `test_create_user` sends a `POST` request to create a user and verifies the response.
- o `test_get_users` sends a `GET` request to retrieve all users and checks if the response is correct.

4. **Running Tests**: To run the tests, simply execute:

```bash
bash
```

```
pytest test_app.py
```

Output: If everything is working, you should see output similar to this:

```bash
bash
```

```
2 passed in 0.12 seconds
```

Best Practices for Flask Testing:

- **Test in isolation**: Ensure that your tests don't rely on external systems (e.g., databases, APIs) by mocking or using a test database.

- **Test different HTTP methods**: Test `GET`, `POST`, `PUT`, and `DELETE` methods for full coverage of your endpoints.
- **Check status codes and content**: Always check the status code, content type, and data returned by the API.

13.2 Testing with Django Rest Framework

Django Rest Framework (DRF) integrates testing seamlessly with Django's testing tools. DRF provides a set of utilities to help test API views and serializers.

Setting Up Testing in Django

1. **Create Test Cases in Django**: Django has a built-in testing framework that extends Python's `unittest`. DRF also includes test mixins that make it easy to test API endpoints.
2. **Write Test Cases for Your API Endpoints**: Let's write tests for a simple `User` API in DRF.

   Example Django App (`models.py`):

   ```python
   python


   from django.db import models


   class User(models.Model):
   ```

```python
    username                          =
models.CharField(max_length=100)
    email = models.EmailField(unique=True)

    def __str__(self):
        return self.username
```

Serializers (`serializers.py`):

python

```python
from rest_framework import serializers
from .models import User

class
UserSerializer(serializers.ModelSerialize
r):
    class Meta:
        model = User
        fields   =   ['id',   'username',
'email']
```

Views (`views.py`):

python

```python
from rest_framework.views import APIView
from     rest_framework.response     import
Response
from rest_framework import status
```

```python
from .models import User
from .serializers import UserSerializer

class UserList(APIView):
    def get(self, request):
        users = User.objects.all()
        serializer = UserSerializer(users,
many=True)
        return Response(serializer.data)

    def post(self, request):
        serializer                      =
UserSerializer(data=request.data)
        if serializer.is_valid():
            serializer.save()
            return
Response(serializer.data,
status=status.HTTP_201_CREATED)
        return Response(serializer.errors,
status=status.HTTP_400_BAD_REQUEST)
```

Test Case for API Endpoints (tests.py):

python

```python
from django.test import TestCase
from rest_framework.test import APIClient
from rest_framework import status

class UserApiTests(TestCase):
```

```python
def setUp(self):
    self.client = APIClient()

def test_create_user(self):
    url = '/api/users/'
    data = {'username': 'john',
'email': 'john@example.com'}
    response = self.client.post(url,
data, format='json')

self.assertEqual(response.status_code,
status.HTTP_201_CREATED)

self.assertEqual(response.data['username'
], 'john')

def test_get_users(self):
    url = '/api/users/'
    self.client.post('/api/users/',
{'username': 'john', 'email':
'john@example.com'}, format='json')
    response = self.client.get(url)

self.assertEqual(response.status_code,
status.HTTP_200_OK)

self.assertEqual(len(response.data), 1)
```

```
self.assertEqual(response.data[0]['userna
me'], 'john')
```

- o `APIClient` is used to simulate HTTP requests in Django tests.
- o `test_create_user` tests the `POST` method to create a user.
- o `test_get_users` tests the `GET` method to retrieve all users.

3. **Running the Tests**: You can run the Django tests by executing:

```bash
```

```
python manage.py test
```

Output: Django will execute the test cases and report the results:

```bash
```

```
2 tests passed in 0.13 seconds
```

Best Practices for Django Testing:

- **Test both views and serializers**: Ensure that both the API views and the serializers work as expected.

- **Use fixtures for setting up test data**: You can use Django's setUp method or fixtures to set up the initial data for your tests.

- **Check both status codes and response data**: Verify that both the HTTP status codes and the data returned match your expectations.

13.3 Debugging Techniques

Debugging is an essential skill for resolving issues in your application. Both Flask and Django have powerful tools and techniques for identifying and fixing bugs in your API.

Debugging in Flask

Flask has built-in support for debugging in development mode. When you run Flask in **debug mode**, it provides detailed error messages, a stack trace, and an interactive debugger in the browser.

1. **Enable Debug Mode**: You can enable Flask's debugging by setting debug=True when running the app:

python

```
if __name__ == '__main__':
    app.run(debug=True)
```

2. **Using Flask's Debugger**: When an error occurs in your app, Flask displays the error in the browser along with a stack trace. You can click on the error trace to inspect variables and navigate through the call stack.

3. **Logging**: Flask provides the ability to log messages. You can add logging to capture critical information about your app's behavior:

```python
import logging
app.logger.setLevel(logging.DEBUG)
app.logger.debug("This    is    a    debug
message")
```

Debugging in Django

Django also has a powerful debugging system that includes detailed error pages and logging. Here's how to debug effectively in Django.

1. **Enable Debug Mode**: Set `DEBUG = True` in your `settings.py` to enable Django's debug mode, which will display detailed error messages when something goes wrong.

2. **Django Debug Toolbar**: The **Django Debug Toolbar** is a great tool for debugging and inspecting Django applications. Install it using:

```bash
bash
```

```bash
pip install django-debug-toolbar
```

Then, add `'debug_toolbar'` to your `INSTALLED_APPS` and include the toolbar middleware in `MIDDLEWARE`:

```python
python
```

```python
MIDDLEWARE = [

'debug_toolbar.middleware.DebugToolbarMiddleware',
    # Other middlewares...
]
```

3. **Logging**: Django's logging system can capture errors and provide insights into your application's behavior. Configure logging in `settings.py` to capture messages:

```python
python
```

```python
LOGGING = {
    'version': 1,
    'disable_existing_loggers': False,
    'handlers': {
        'file': {
            'level': 'DEBUG',
```

```
            'class':
'logging.FileHandler',
            'filename':
'django_debug.log',
        },
    },
    'loggers': {
        'django': {
            'handlers': ['file'],
            'level': 'DEBUG',
            'propagate': True,
        },
    },
}
```

Summary of Key Concepts

In this chapter, we:

- Learned how to **unit test** API endpoints in **Flask** using **pytest** and Flask's test client.
- Explored how to write test cases for your API endpoints in **Django** using **Django Rest Framework** and **APIClient**.
- Discussed effective **debugging techniques** in Flask and Django, including using Flask's built-in debugger, the **Django Debug Toolbar**, and logging.

160

Unit testing ensures that your API works as expected, while debugging tools help you identify and resolve issues during development. In the next chapters, we will explore further topics such as API rate limiting, pagination, and security measures to enhance the robustness of your API.

CHAPTER 14

DEPLOYING YOUR API TO THE CLOUD

Once you've built and tested your API, the next step is deployment, which makes your API accessible to users and clients. In this chapter, we'll cover how to deploy APIs built with **Flask** and **Django** to the cloud. We'll also compare popular deployment platforms like **Heroku**, **AWS**, and **DigitalOcean**, and show you how to deploy your APIs on these platforms.

14.1 Choosing a Deployment Platform

When deciding where to deploy your API, there are several cloud platforms to choose from. The right choice depends on factors like cost, scalability, ease of use, and the features you need. Below is a comparison of three popular platforms: **Heroku**, **AWS**, and **DigitalOcean**.

1. Heroku

- **Overview**: Heroku is a **Platform-as-a-Service (PaaS)** that allows you to deploy web applications quickly and easily. It abstracts away much of the complexity of server management and provides a simple interface for deploying applications.

- **Pros**:
  - **Easy to use**: Heroku is ideal for developers who want a simple deployment process.
  - **Free tier**: Heroku offers a free tier with limited resources (great for small projects and testing).
  - **Great for beginners**: With little setup required, Heroku is a great platform for beginners.
- **Cons**:
  - **Limited flexibility**: Since Heroku abstracts away server management, it can be less customizable for advanced configurations.
  - **Scalability limitations**: Heroku's free tier and low-cost options can be limiting for high-traffic applications.

2. AWS (Amazon Web Services)

- **Overview**: AWS is one of the most widely used cloud platforms, providing a wide range of services, from compute power to databases and machine learning. AWS offers more control and flexibility compared to Heroku.
- **Pros**:
  - **Scalability**: AWS allows for massive scalability, which is ideal for applications that need to handle high traffic.

163

- o **Customization**: AWS offers a lot of flexibility and control over your deployment.
- o **Wide range of services**: You can integrate with other AWS services like RDS (for databases), Lambda (for serverless computing), and S3 (for storage).

- **Cons**:
  - o **Complexity**: AWS can be overwhelming for beginners, with a steep learning curve and a lot of setup required.
  - o **Cost**: AWS is more expensive than simpler platforms like Heroku, especially as your application scales.

3. DigitalOcean

- **Overview**: DigitalOcean is a cloud infrastructure provider that offers simple virtual private servers (called **Droplets**). It's a great choice for developers who want more control over their environment, but without the complexity of AWS.
- **Pros**:
  - o **Simple and affordable**: DigitalOcean is relatively inexpensive and provides a user-friendly interface.
  - o **Scalability**: DigitalOcean offers good scalability, though it's not as extensive as AWS.

164

- o **Good for small to medium applications**: DigitalOcean is great for startups and small to medium-sized applications that need more control than Heroku.
- **Cons**:
  - o **Less managed services**: While you get more control over your infrastructure, you also need to manage more aspects of your app compared to PaaS options like Heroku.
  - o **Limited advanced features**: If you need advanced cloud computing features (e.g., machine learning services, complex databases), AWS might be a better choice.

Conclusion:

- If you want the easiest, quickest deployment with minimal setup, **Heroku** is a great choice.
- If you need full control, flexibility, and scalability for your application, **AWS** is ideal, especially for large applications.
- For a middle ground with some flexibility but still manageable, **DigitalOcean** is a good option.

14.2 Deploying Flask on Heroku

Deploying a **Flask** API to **Heroku** is straightforward. Here's a step-by-step guide to get your Flask app up and running on Heroku.

Step 1: Install Heroku CLI

First, you need to install the **Heroku CLI** on your machine.

- Visit Heroku CLI and follow the installation instructions for your operating system.

Step 2: Create a Flask App

If you haven't already, create a simple Flask app (e.g., app.py).

python

```
from flask import Flask

app = Flask(__name__)

@app.route('/')
def home():
    return "Hello, Heroku!"

if __name__ == '__main__':
    app.run(debug=True)
```

Step 3: Set Up Git

Heroku uses Git for deployment. If your project is not already in a Git repository, initialize one:

bash

```
git init
git add .
git commit -m "Initial commit"
```

Step 4: Create a requirements.txt File

Create a requirements.txt file to specify the dependencies your app needs:

bash

```
Flask==2.0.1
gunicorn==20.1.0
```

gunicorn is a Python WSGI HTTP server that Heroku uses to run your app.

Step 5: Create a Procfile

A Procfile tells Heroku how to run your app. Create a file called Procfile (no file extension) in the root of your project with the following content:

makefile

web: gunicorn app:app

This tells Heroku to use `gunicorn` to run the Flask app defined in `app.py`.

Step 6: Log In to Heroku

Log in to your Heroku account via the CLI:

bash

heroku login

Step 7: Create a Heroku App

Create a new Heroku app:

bash

heroku create your-app-name

This command will create a new app on Heroku and add a remote Git repository for deployment.

Step 8: Deploy to Heroku

Push your code to Heroku:

bash

```
git push heroku master
```

Heroku will install the dependencies and deploy the app. After deployment, Heroku will provide a URL to access your app.

Step 9: Open Your App

To open your app in a browser:

```
bash
```

```
heroku open
```

14.3 Deploying Django on AWS

Deploying a **Django** app with **PostgreSQL** on **AWS EC2** (Elastic Compute Cloud) gives you full control over your server and database. Below is a step-by-step guide to deploying a **Django Rest Framework API** on AWS.

Step 1: Set Up an EC2 Instance

1. Log in to your **AWS Console**.
2. Navigate to **EC2** and click **Launch Instance**.
3. Choose an **Amazon Machine Image (AMI)** (e.g., Ubuntu).
4. Select an instance type (e.g., **t2.micro** for the free tier).

5. Configure the instance settings (default settings should work for testing purposes).

6. Create a **key pair** for SSH access.

7. Launch the instance and take note of the **public IP address**.

Step 2: SSH into Your EC2 Instance

Use SSH to connect to your EC2 instance.

bash

```
ssh -i "your-key.pem" ubuntu@your-ec2-ip
```

Step 3: Install Dependencies

Once connected to the EC2 instance, install the necessary dependencies:

bash

```
sudo apt update
sudo apt install python3-pip python3-dev libpq-dev
sudo apt install nginx
```

Install **virtualenv** and **PostgreSQL**:

bash

```bash
pip3 install virtualenv
sudo apt install postgresql postgresql-contrib
```

Step 4: Set Up PostgreSQL Database

Create a PostgreSQL database and user for your Django app:

bash

```
sudo -u postgres psql
CREATE DATABASE mydb;
CREATE USER myuser WITH PASSWORD 'mypassword';
ALTER ROLE myuser SET client_encoding TO 'utf8';
ALTER ROLE myuser SET default_transaction_isolation TO 'read committed';
ALTER ROLE myuser SET timezone TO 'UTC';
GRANT ALL PRIVILEGES ON DATABASE mydb TO myuser;
```

Step 5: Set Up Your Django Application

1. Clone or upload your Django project to the EC2 instance.
2. Create a **virtual environment** and install the necessary packages:

bash

```
virtualenv venv
source venv/bin/activate
pip install -r requirements.txt
```

3. Update the DATABASES setting in your settings.py to use PostgreSQL:

```python
python
```

```python
DATABASES = {
    'default': {
        'ENGINE':
'django.db.backends.postgresql',
        'NAME': 'mydb',
        'USER': 'myuser',
        'PASSWORD': 'mypassword',
        'HOST': 'localhost',
        'PORT': '5432',
    }
}
```

4. Run the migrations:

```bash
bash
```

```bash
python manage.py migrate
```

Step 6: Configure Nginx and Gunicorn

Install **Gunicorn** and **Nginx** to serve your Django application:

```bash
bash
```

```bash
pip install gunicorn
```

172

Create a **Gunicorn** service to run the Django app and configure **Nginx** to act as a reverse proxy.

Step 7: Start Your Application

Finally, you can run your Django app with Gunicorn:

```bash
```

```
gunicorn --workers 3 myproject.wsgi:application
```

Configure **Nginx** to serve the app by editing its configuration files.

Summary of Key Concepts

In this chapter, we:

- **Compared deployment platforms** like **Heroku**, **AWS**, and **DigitalOcean**, discussing their advantages and use cases.
- **Deployed a Flask API to Heroku**, including setting up the app, configuring necessary files (`requirements.txt`, `Procfile`), and pushing to Heroku.

- **Deployed a Django Rest Framework API to AWS**, with steps to set up an EC2 instance, install dependencies, configure PostgreSQL, and set up Gunicorn and Nginx.

Cloud deployment makes your API accessible to the world, and the choice of platform will depend on your needs for control, scalability, and ease of use. In the next chapters, we'll look at additional advanced topics like API rate limiting, caching, and security best practices.

CHAPTER 15

INTRODUCTION TO WEBSOCKETS

As applications grow increasingly interactive, the need for real-time communication has become more crucial. **WebSockets** enable real-time, bidirectional communication between clients and servers, making them ideal for applications like live chats, live sports feeds, notifications, and more. In this chapter, we'll explore **WebSockets** and how they can be used to create real-time features in both **Flask** and **Django**.

15.1 Understanding WebSockets and Real-Time APIs

What are WebSockets?

WebSockets provide a full-duplex communication channel over a single, long-lived connection. This allows data to be sent and received between the client and the server in real-time, without the need for repeatedly opening new HTTP connections.

In traditional HTTP communication, the client makes a request to the server, and the server responds. This is a **request-response** model. However, **WebSockets** create a persistent connection that allows either side to send messages at any time.

Why WebSockets for Real-Time Data?

WebSockets are ideal for applications that need real-time updates. These applications require low-latency communication, where the server can push updates to clients as soon as new data becomes available, without waiting for the client to request it.

- **Real-Time Chat Applications**: Chat apps need to update the chat window with new messages without requiring the user to refresh or manually fetch new data.
- **Live Sports Scores**: WebSockets enable real-time updates for live sports scores, allowing users to get instant notifications as the game progresses.
- **Collaborative Applications**: Apps like Google Docs that require real-time collaboration benefit from WebSockets, enabling instant updates as users edit a document.

How WebSockets Work

1. **Connection Establishment**: A client sends a WebSocket handshake request to the server over HTTP.
2. **Protocol Upgrade**: If the server supports WebSockets, it replies with a WebSocket handshake response, upgrading the protocol from HTTP to WebSocket.
3. **Data Transfer**: Once the WebSocket connection is established, both the client and server can send and receive messages freely until the connection is closed.

Example of WebSocket Communication:

- **Client**: Sends a message to the server: "Hello Server!"
- **Server**: Responds in real-time with "Hello Client!"

This communication is instantaneous, allowing both sides to talk to each other without delay.

15.2 Building Real-Time Features with Flask-SocketIO

In Flask, you can use the **Flask-SocketIO** extension to add WebSocket support to your app. Flask-SocketIO allows you to easily create real-time features like chat applications.

Step 1: Install Flask-SocketIO

First, install the necessary dependencies:

bash

```
pip install flask-socketio
```

Step 2: Create a Simple Chat App

Here's a basic example of a real-time chat application using Flask and Flask-SocketIO:

1. **Flask App Setup** (app.py):

```python
python

from flask import Flask, render_template
from flask_socketio import SocketIO, send

app = Flask(__name__)
socketio = SocketIO(app)

@app.route('/')
def index():
    return render_template('index.html')

@socketio.on('message')
def handle_message(msg):
    print('Message received: ' + msg)
    send(msg, broadcast=True)

if __name__ == '__main__':
    socketio.run(app, debug=True)
```

2. **HTML Template for Chat UI**
(templates/index.html):

```html
html

<!DOCTYPE html>
<html>
<head>
    <title>Real-Time Chat</title>
```

178

```
    <script
src="https://cdnjs.cloudflare.com/ajax/li
bs/socket.io/4.0.1/socket.io.min.js"></sc
ript>
</head>
<body>
    <h1>Chat Room</h1>
    <input    type="text"    id="message"
placeholder="Type your message">
    <button
onclick="sendMessage()">Send</button>
    <ul id="messages"></ul>

    <script>
        var socket = io();

        socket.on('message', function(msg)
{
            var        messages        =
document.getElementById('messages');
            var         li         =
document.createElement('li');
            li.textContent = msg;
            messages.appendChild(li);
        });

        function sendMessage() {
            var        msg        =
document.getElementById('message').value;
```

179

```
                socket.send(msg);

document.getElementById('message').value =
'';
        }
    </script>
</body>
</html>
```

Explanation:

- **SocketIO Instance**: We initialize Flask-SocketIO with `socketio = SocketIO(app)`.
- **handle_message Function**: When a message is sent, the server receives it, prints it to the console, and broadcasts it to all connected clients.
- **Client-Side**: In the HTML file, we use Socket.IO's JavaScript client to send and receive messages in real time.

Step 3: Running the Flask App

To start the app, run the following command:

```bash
```

```
python app.py
```

When you visit `http://localhost:5000/` in a browser, you can start typing messages. These messages will be broadcast to all connected clients in real time.

15.3 WebSockets with Django Channels

For **Django**, you can use **Django Channels**, an extension that adds support for WebSockets, HTTP2, and other asynchronous protocols.

Step 1: Install Django Channels

1. Install the necessary packages for **Django Channels**:

    bash

    ```
    pip install channels
    ```

2. Install **Channels Redis** if you want to support WebSocket connections over multiple instances (optional, but recommended for production):

    bash

    ```
    pip install channels_redis
    ```

Step 2: Configure Django Channels

1. **Update `settings.py`**: Add channels to INSTALLED_APPS and set the ASGI application to channels.routing.application.

   python

   ```python
   INSTALLED_APPS = [
       # Other apps...
       'channels',
   ]

   ASGI_APPLICATION =
   'myproject.asgi.application'
   ```

2. **Create `asgi.py` in your project root directory**: This file tells Django to use Channels for handling WebSockets.

   python

   ```python
   import os
   from django.core.asgi import import
   get_asgi_application
   from channels.routing import
   ProtocolTypeRouter, URLRouter
   from channels.auth import
   AuthMiddlewareStack
   ```

```
from        channels.websocket        import
WebsocketConsumer


os.environ.setdefault('DJANGO_SETTINGS_MO
DULE', 'myproject.settings')


application = ProtocolTypeRouter({
    "http": get_asgi_application(),
    "websocket": AuthMiddlewareStack(
        URLRouter([
            # Define    URL   routing   for
WebSocket connections
            #    e.g.,    path("ws/chat/",
ChatConsumer.as_asgi()),
        ])
    ),
})
```

Step 3: Implement a Chat Consumer

A **Consumer** in Django Channels handles WebSocket connections. Let's create a simple chat consumer:

1. **Create consumers.py**: In your app directory, create a consumers.py file:

```
python


import json
```

```python
from channels.generic.websocket import
AsyncWebsocketConsumer

class
ChatConsumer(AsyncWebsocketConsumer):
    async def connect(self):
        self.room_name = "chatroom"
        self.room_group_name                =
f'chat_{self.room_name}'

        # Join room group
        await
self.channel_layer.group_add(
            self.room_group_name,
            self.channel_name
        )

        await self.accept()

    async        def       disconnect(self,
close_code):
        # Leave room group
        await
self.channel_layer.group_discard(
            self.room_group_name,
            self.channel_name
        )

    # Receive message from WebSocket
```

```python
    async def receive(self, text_data):
        text_data_json                =
json.loads(text_data)
        message                       =
text_data_json['message']

        # Send message to room group
        await
self.channel_layer.group_send(
            self.room_group_name,
            {
                'type': 'chat_message',
                'message': message
            }
        )

    # Receive message from room group
    async def chat_message(self, event):
        message = event['message']

        # Send message to WebSocket
        await
self.send(text_data=json.dumps({
            'message': message
        }))
```

Step 4: Routing WebSocket Requests

Define URL routing for WebSocket connections by modifying
routing.py:

```python
python

from django.urls import re_path
from . import consumers

websocket_urlpatterns = [
    re_path(r'ws/chat/',
consumers.ChatConsumer.as_asgi()),
]
```

Then, link this routing in `asgi.py`:

```python
python

from channels.routing import ProtocolTypeRouter,
URLRouter
from channels.auth import AuthMiddlewareStack
from . import routing

application = ProtocolTypeRouter({
    "http": get_asgi_application(),
    "websocket": AuthMiddlewareStack(
        URLRouter(
            routing.websocket_urlpatterns
        )
    ),
})
```

Step 5: Running the Django Channels Application

Finally, to run Django Channels, use **Daphne** or **Uvicorn** as the ASGI server.

bash

```
pip install daphne
daphne myproject.asgi:application
```

This will start your server with WebSocket support. You can now implement a front-end for real-time communication in your Django app using WebSockets.

Summary of Key Concepts

In this chapter, we:

- Discussed **WebSockets** and their importance for building real-time features in modern applications like chat apps, live sports, and collaborative platforms.
- Built a **real-time chat app with Flask** using **Flask-SocketIO**, which allowed for easy integration of WebSockets.

- Explored how to build real-time features in **Django** using **Django Channels**, which provides powerful support for WebSockets and asynchronous protocols.

WebSockets provide a powerful way to add real-time communication to your API, and with the knowledge of both Flask-SocketIO and Django Channels, you're equipped to build interactive, responsive applications. In the next chapters, we'll dive deeper into securing your API and handling more advanced real-time scenarios.

CHAPTER 16

CACHING AND PERFORMANCE OPTIMIZATION

When building APIs, performance is crucial. Users expect fast responses, especially when interacting with web services that handle large datasets or high traffic. **Caching** is one of the most effective ways to improve API performance by storing the results of expensive computations or frequently requested data, reducing the need to repeatedly fetch or compute the same data.

In this chapter, we'll cover the importance of caching, demonstrate how to integrate **Redis** for caching in **Flask**, and explore performance optimization techniques for **Django** APIs, including query optimization.

16.1 Why Caching is Important for APIs

What is Caching?

Caching is the process of temporarily storing copies of data in memory (or other fast storage) to speed up subsequent requests. Instead of fetching or computing the same data over and over again, the application retrieves it from the cache, which is much faster.

189

Why is Caching Important?

- **Improves Performance**: By reducing the number of times the server has to process the same data or query the database, caching significantly speeds up response times.
- **Reduces Load on Backend Systems**: Caching reduces the number of requests to the database or external services, helping to prevent system overload.
- **Saves Resources**: Caching avoids unnecessary computations or data retrieval, saving computational resources and bandwidth.

Real-World Examples Where Caching Improves Performance

1. **E-commerce Sites**: For e-commerce platforms with thousands of products, caching the product details (price, description, image) ensures that frequent requests for the same products are served quickly without querying the database each time.

2. **Weather APIs**: For weather services, caching weather data for specific locations for a short period (e.g., 10 minutes) avoids redundant requests to external weather APIs, which often have rate limits and slower response times.

3. **Social Media Feeds**: For social media platforms, caching user feeds ensures that users see content quickly without querying the database each time the feed is requested.

190

Caching Strategies

- **Time-based Expiration**: Cache data for a specified period. For example, weather data might be cached for 10 minutes.
- **Lazy Loading**: Only cache data when it's requested for the first time.
- **Cache Invalidation**: Ensure that cached data is updated or removed when the underlying data changes (e.g., when a product price changes).

16.2 Using Redis with Flask

Redis is a powerful in-memory key-value store commonly used for caching. It's fast and efficient, making it an ideal choice for improving the performance of Flask APIs.

Setting Up Redis with Flask

1. **Install Redis**: First, install the **Redis** package and the **Flask-Redis** extension.

   bash

   ```
   pip install redis flask-redis
   ```

2. **Install Redis Server**: You'll need to have a **Redis server** running. You can either install Redis locally or use a cloud-based Redis service (e.g., **Redis Labs** or **AWS Elasticache**).

   o **Install Redis on Ubuntu**:

   ```bash
   bash

   sudo apt update
   sudo apt install redis-server
   ```

3. **Configure Flask to Use Redis**: In your Flask app, initialize the Redis connection.

   Flask App with Redis (app.py):

   ```python
   python

   from flask import Flask, jsonify
   from flask_redis import Redis

   app = Flask(__name__)
   app.config['REDIS_URL']                    =
   "redis://localhost:6379/0"   # URL of the
   Redis server
   redis = Redis(app)

   @app.route('/data')
   def get_data():
   ```

```
# Try to get cached data
cached_data = redis.get('my_data')
if cached_data:
    return         jsonify({'data':
cached_data.decode('utf-8'),      'source':
'cache'})

    # If not cached, fetch new data
(simulate with a long operation)
    data = "Expensive Data Computation
Result"

    # Cache the data for 60 seconds
    redis.setex('my_data', 60, data)

    return     jsonify({'data':      data,
'source': 'database'})

if __name__ == '__main__':
    app.run(debug=True)
```

Explanation:

- `redis.get('my_data')`: Attempts to retrieve data from the cache.
- `redis.setex('my_data', 60, data)`: Stores data in the cache for 60 seconds.
- The first time the /data endpoint is called, the server simulates fetching data from a database and caches it for

193

future requests. Subsequent requests within 60 seconds will return the cached data.

Step 3: Running the Flask App with Redis

1. **Start Redis Server**:

bash

```
redis-server
```

2. **Run Flask App**:

bash

```
python app.py
```

3. **Testing**:
   - When you access `http://localhost:5000/data` for the first time, it will return data from the simulated database.
   - On subsequent requests within 60 seconds, the response will be served from the cache.

16.3 Optimizing Queries in Django

In **Django**, the database layer is key to application performance. Poorly optimized queries can significantly slow down your API. Here are some techniques to optimize queries in **Django Rest Framework (DRF)** APIs.

1. Use `select_related` and `prefetch_related`

Django's ORM provides `select_related` and `prefetch_related` to optimize database queries by reducing the number of queries made when fetching related objects.

- **`select_related`**: Used for **foreign key** and **one-to-one** relationships. It performs a SQL join and retrieves the related data in a single query.
- **`prefetch_related`**: Used for **many-to-many** and reverse **foreign key** relationships. It performs separate queries but minimizes the number of queries.

Example: Optimizing Database Queries in DRF

Consider a scenario where you have `User` and `Profile` models, where `Profile` has a foreign key to `User`.

python

```
class User(models.Model):
```

```
    username = models.CharField(max_length=100)

class Profile(models.Model):
    user          =          models.ForeignKey(User,
on_delete=models.CASCADE)
    bio = models.TextField()
```

Without optimization, fetching a user and their profile might result in **N+1 queries**, where one query is made to fetch all users and then another query for each user's profile.

python

```
# Inefficient query
users = User.objects.all()
for user in users:
    print(user.profile.bio)    # Results in an
additional query for each user
```

Using **select_related**:

python

```
# Optimized query using select_related
users                                          =
User.objects.select_related('profile').all()
for user in users:
    print(user.profile.bio)    # No  additional
queries
```

2. Use Indexing and Database Optimization

Indexing is an essential optimization for frequently queried fields. In Django, you can add indexes to your models to speed up query performance:

```python
python

class User(models.Model):
    username = models.CharField(max_length=100,
db_index=True)   # Adds index to 'username'
```

3. Database Caching with Django

You can cache database query results using Django's caching framework, which integrates well with **Redis**.

1. **Install Redis for Django**:

```bash
bash

pip install django-redis
```

2. **Configure Redis Caching** in settings.py:

```python
python

CACHES = {
    'default': {
```

```
        'BACKEND':
'django_redis.cache.RedisCache',
        'LOCATION':
'redis://127.0.0.1:6379/1',  # Use Redis
        'OPTIONS': {
            'CLIENT_CLASS':
'django_redis.client.DefaultClient'
            }
        }
    }
```

3. **Cache Query Results**: In your views, use `cache_page` decorator or manually cache the result of expensive queries.

```python
python

from    django.views.decorators.cache    import
cache_page
from django.shortcuts import render

@cache_page(60 * 15)  # Cache for 15 minutes
def expensive_view(request):
    # Some expensive database query
    data = some_expensive_database_query()
    return    render(request,    'template.html',
{'data': data})
```

4. Use Database Transactions

Django supports **atomic transactions**, which help avoid multiple database hits when performing write operations. You can group multiple database operations into a single transaction:

```python
from django.db import transaction

@transaction.atomic
def create_user_profile(user_data, profile_data):
    user = User.objects.create(**user_data)
    profile = Profile.objects.create(user=user, **profile_data)
    return user, profile
```

Summary of Key Concepts

In this chapter, we:

- Discussed the importance of **caching** for improving API performance, including real-world examples where caching reduces response times and database load.
- Demonstrated how to **integrate Redis** with Flask for caching API responses, making your Flask APIs faster and more efficient.

- Explored techniques for **optimizing database queries** in Django, including using `select_related` and `prefetch_related` to reduce the number of queries and using database caching to store frequently accessed data.

Caching and query optimization are essential for ensuring that your APIs can handle high traffic efficiently, providing fast responses and reducing the strain on your backend systems. In the next chapters, we will explore additional performance optimizations and security practices for APIs.

CHAPTER 17

HANDLING RATE LIMITING AND THROTTLING

Rate limiting and throttling are critical techniques for ensuring the stability, security, and scalability of your APIs. They help control the amount of traffic that can access your API, preventing abuse and reducing the risk of service outages. In this chapter, we will explore **rate limiting** and **throttling** in both **Flask** and **Django**, and demonstrate how to implement these techniques to protect your services.

17.1 Understanding Rate Limiting in APIs

What is Rate Limiting?

Rate limiting refers to the practice of restricting the number of requests a user (or client) can make to an API within a specified time window (e.g., 100 requests per minute). This ensures that no single user can overwhelm the API, keeping it accessible for everyone.

Why Rate Limiting is Crucial for Protecting Your Services

1. **Preventing Abuse**:

- o **DDoS Attacks**: Rate limiting helps mitigate **Distributed Denial of Service (DDoS)** attacks, where malicious users flood the API with an excessive number of requests to disrupt the service.
- o **Bot Protection**: It prevents automated scripts or bots from sending too many requests, which could exploit the system.

2. **Ensuring Fair Usage**:
   - o By enforcing limits, you ensure that no user can monopolize the API, allowing for fair access among all users.
   - o This is particularly important for free-tier users who might be abusing the service.

3. **Improving Performance**:
   - o By limiting requests, you reduce the load on the server, allowing it to serve legitimate users more efficiently.

4. **Protecting Resources**:
   - o Rate limiting helps prevent overuse of limited resources, such as database queries, third-party API calls, or computational power.

Common Rate Limiting Strategies:

- **Global Rate Limiting**: Limits requests for all users across the API.

- **User-based Rate Limiting**: Limits requests for each individual user, usually identified by their **API key** or **IP address**.
- **IP-based Rate Limiting**: Applies rate limits based on the user's IP address, often used to limit traffic from a single source.

Rate limits are often defined in terms of **requests per time window** (e.g., 100 requests per minute, 500 requests per day).

17.2 Implementing Rate Limiting in Flask

In Flask, you can implement rate limiting using the **Flask-Limiter** extension. It provides a simple way to restrict the number of requests from each client within a time frame.

Setting Up Flask-Limiter

1. **Install Flask-Limiter**: Install the necessary package via pip:

bash

```
pip install Flask-Limiter
```

2. **Create a Simple Flask App with Rate Limiting**

Here's an example of implementing rate limiting in a Flask app using Flask-Limiter:

python

```python
from flask import Flask, jsonify
from flask_limiter import Limiter
from           flask_limiter.util          import
get_remote_address

app = Flask(__name__)
limiter              =              Limiter(app,
key_func=get_remote_address)

# Apply rate limit: 5 requests per minute per IP
@app.route('/api/resource')
@limiter.limit("5 per minute")
def resource():
    return jsonify(message="This   is   a   rate-
limited resource.")

if __name__ == '__main__':
    app.run(debug=True)
```

Explanation:

- **Flask-Limiter Setup**: The `Limiter` instance is created and linked to the Flask app. The `key_func=get_remote_address` tells Flask-Limiter to limit based on the user's IP address.

204

- **@limiter.limit("5 per minute")**: This decorator applies rate limiting to the /api/resource route, allowing only 5 requests per minute per user (IP address).
- If the limit is exceeded, Flask-Limiter automatically responds with a 429 Too Many Requests status.

Step 3: Running the Flask App

To test the rate limiting, start your Flask app:

bash

```
python app.py
```

When accessing http://localhost:5000/api/resource, the user can only make 5 requests per minute. After that, they'll receive a 429 status code until the next time window.

17.3 Throttling in Django

In Django, you can use **Django Rest Framework (DRF)**'s built-in **throttling** classes to implement rate limiting. DRF provides several built-in throttling classes, such as AnonRateThrottle, UserRateThrottle, and ScopedRateThrottle, which can be used to control the rate of API requests.

205

Setting Up Throttling in Django

1. **Enable Throttling in Django Settings**: First, you need to add throttling settings to your Django `settings.py` file:

```python
REST_FRAMEWORK = {
    'DEFAULT_THROTTLE_CLASSES': [

'rest_framework.throttling.UserRateThrottle',

'rest_framework.throttling.AnonRateThrottle',
    ],
    'DEFAULT_THROTTLE_RATES': {
        'user': '5/hour',  # 5 requests per hour for logged-in users
        'anon': '2/hour',  # 2 requests per hour for anonymous users
    },
}
```

2. **Create a Simple Django API with Throttling**

Here's an example of a Django Rest Framework view with rate limiting:

1. Define the API View:

python

```python
from rest_framework.views import APIView
from rest_framework.response import Response
from rest_framework.permissions import IsAuthenticated
from rest_framework.throttling import UserRateThrottle

class ResourceView(APIView):
    throttle_classes = [UserRateThrottle]

    def get(self, request):
        return Response({"message": "This is a rate-limited resource."})
```

2. Set Up URL Routing: In urls.py, add the URL for the ResourceView:

python

```python
from django.urls import path
from .views import ResourceView

urlpatterns = [
    path('api/resource/',
ResourceView.as_view(), name='resource'),
]
```

Explanation:

- **Throttle Classes**: `UserRateThrottle` limits requests for logged-in users to a defined number of requests per time period (as configured in `settings.py`).
- **throttle_classes**: This attribute applies the `UserRateThrottle` to the `ResourceView`. You can also use `AnonRateThrottle` for anonymous users or `ScopedRateThrottle` for different endpoints.

Step 3: Running the Django App

Once your Django app is running, any requests to `/api/resource/` will be throttled based on the rate limits defined in the `settings.py` file.

To start the Django development server:

bash

```
python manage.py runserver
```

- **Logged-in users**: Can make 5 requests per hour (as per the `user` throttle in `settings.py`).
- **Anonymous users**: Can make 2 requests per hour.

17.4 Advanced Throttling Techniques

Both **Flask-Limiter** and **Django Rest Framework** provide advanced options for customizing rate limiting and throttling behavior.

1. Custom Throttling in DRF

You can define your own custom throttling classes by extending `BaseThrottle` in **DRF**.

python

```python
from rest_framework.throttling import BaseThrottle

class CustomRateThrottle(BaseThrottle):
    def allow_request(self, request, view):
        # Define custom throttling logic here
        return True  # or False if request is throttled

    def wait(self):
        return 60  # Return time to wait before next request in seconds
```

2. Scoped Rate Limiting

You can apply rate limiting to specific **views** or **endpoints** by using `ScopedRateThrottle`. This allows for more granular control over rate limits for different parts of your application.

python

```python
REST_FRAMEWORK = {
    'DEFAULT_THROTTLE_CLASSES': [

'rest_framework.throttling.ScopedRateThrottle',
    ],
    'DEFAULT_THROTTLE_RATES': {
        'resource': '5/hour',   # Specific rate
limit for this scope
    },
}
```

Then, in your view:

python

```python
from rest_framework.views import APIView
from     rest_framework.permissions     import
IsAuthenticated
from     rest_framework.throttling     import
ScopedRateThrottle

class ResourceView(APIView):
```

```
throttle_classes = [ScopedRateThrottle]
throttle_scope = 'resource'

def get(self, request):
    return   Response({"message":   "Scoped
rate-limited resource."})
```

This limits the number of requests to `/api/resource/` to 5 per hour for each client.

Summary of Key Concepts

In this chapter, we:

- Discussed **rate limiting** and **throttling** and why they are important for protecting your API from abuse, ensuring fair usage, and improving performance.
- Implemented **rate limiting in Flask** using **Flask-Limiter** to limit the number of requests a user can make within a specified time window.
- Explored **throttling in Django** using **Django Rest Framework**'s built-in throttling classes, like `UserRateThrottle` and `AnonRateThrottle`.
- Covered **advanced throttling techniques**, such as custom throttling classes and scoped rate limiting, to further control how your API handles requests.

Rate limiting and throttling are essential for maintaining the stability and security of your API, particularly as it scales and attracts more users. In the next chapters, we'll delve deeper into additional API security measures and best practices for maintaining API performance and reliability.

CHAPTER 18

SECURING YOUR API

In today's interconnected world, ensuring the security of your API is essential to protect sensitive data and maintain the trust of your users. APIs are often exposed to the internet, making them vulnerable to a variety of attacks. In this chapter, we'll cover **security best practices**, how to protect against **CORS** and **CSRF**, and dive deep into securing your API with **OAuth2** and **OpenID Connect**.

18.1 Security Best Practices

APIs are prone to several types of security vulnerabilities. Following best practices can help mitigate these risks and ensure that your API is secure. Here are some **best practices** to keep in mind when building APIs:

1. Use HTTPS

Always use **HTTPS** (Hypertext Transfer Protocol Secure) for all API communication. HTTPS ensures that data transmitted between the client and the server is encrypted, making it much harder for attackers to intercept or tamper with the data.

- **Why it matters**: Without HTTPS, data (including sensitive user information, passwords, and API keys) can be sent in plain text, which can be intercepted by malicious actors.

2. Implement Strong Authentication

Strong authentication ensures that only authorized users can access your API. Implement **authentication mechanisms** like **JWT (JSON Web Tokens)**, **OAuth2**, or **API keys** to verify the identity of users and ensure secure access.

- **JWT**: Commonly used in stateless APIs, JWT allows clients to authenticate once and use a token to access protected resources.
- **OAuth2**: Ideal for delegating access to resources without exposing user credentials, commonly used in third-party integrations.

3. Rate Limiting

Implement **rate limiting** (discussed in Chapter 17) to control the number of requests a user can make in a given time frame. Rate limiting helps protect against **DDoS attacks** and ensures fair usage of your resources.

4. Input Validation

Validate all incoming data to ensure it matches the expected format. This can help prevent attacks like **SQL injection** and **XSS (Cross-Site Scripting)**, where attackers try to inject malicious data into your application.

- **Example**: If you expect an integer as input, ensure the data is indeed an integer before processing it.

5. Avoid Exposing Sensitive Data

Never expose sensitive information like **API keys**, **passwords**, or **internal server details** in API responses. Always mask or exclude sensitive data when sending responses to clients.

6. Use the Principle of Least Privilege

Ensure that each part of your API has the minimum level of access needed to perform its function. For example, if a user only needs to read data, don't give them write or delete permissions.

7. Regularly Update Dependencies

Ensure that your application and its dependencies are up-to-date. Use dependency management tools to track and automatically update third-party packages to avoid using outdated or insecure libraries.

215

8. Error Handling

Avoid exposing stack traces or sensitive error details to the client. Use general error messages for clients and log detailed errors server-side for debugging.

18.2 CORS and CSRF Protection

Two common security threats in web applications are **CORS (Cross-Origin Resource Sharing)** and **CSRF (Cross-Site Request Forgery)**. Let's go over how to protect your API from these threats.

1. CORS (Cross-Origin Resource Sharing)

CORS is a security feature implemented by web browsers that controls which websites are allowed to make requests to your server. It prevents unauthorized websites from making API requests to your domain.

- **Why it's important**: Without CORS protection, malicious websites could make unauthorized requests to your API on behalf of users, potentially leaking sensitive data.

Implementing CORS in Flask

To implement **CORS** in Flask, you can use the **Flask-CORS** extension:

1. **Install Flask-CORS**:

   bash

   ```bash
   pip install flask-cors
   ```

2. **Enable CORS in Flask**:

   python

   ```python
   from flask import Flask
   from flask_cors import CORS

   app = Flask(__name__)
   CORS(app)  # Enable CORS for all routes

   @app.route('/api/data')
   def get_data():
       return {'data': 'This is some data'}

   if __name__ == '__main__':
       app.run(debug=True)
   ```

217

Implementing CORS in Django

In **Django,** you can use the **django-cors-headers** library to handle CORS:

1. **Install django-cors-headers**:

   bash

   ```
   pip install django-cors-headers
   ```

2. **Add it to `INSTALLED_APPS` and `MIDDLEWARE` in** settings.py:

   python

   ```
   INSTALLED_APPS = [
       'corsheaders',
       # Other apps...
   ]

   MIDDLEWARE = [

   'corsheaders.middleware.CorsMiddleware',

   'django.middleware.common.CommonMiddlewar
   e',
       # Other middleware...
   ]
   ```

```
# Allow all domains to make requests (for
development)
CORS_ALLOW_ALL_ORIGINS = True
```

- **Note**: In production, it's better to restrict access to specific domains by setting `CORS_ALLOWED_ORIGINS` instead of using `CORS_ALLOW_ALL_ORIGINS`.

2. CSRF Protection (Cross-Site Request Forgery)

CSRF is an attack where a malicious site tricks a user into making an unwanted request to your API (e.g., submitting a form on their behalf). CSRF protection prevents unauthorized sites from submitting requests to your API using a user's credentials.

Implementing CSRF Protection in Flask

Flask provides built-in **CSRF** protection with the **Flask-WTF** extension:

1. **Install Flask-WTF**:

   bash

   ```
   pip install Flask-WTF
   ```

2. **Enable CSRF Protection**:

   python

```python
from flask import Flask, render_template,
request
from flask_wtf.csrf import CSRFProtect

app = Flask(__name__)
app.config['SECRET_KEY']              =
'your_secret_key'
csrf = CSRFProtect(app)

@app.route('/submit', methods=['POST'])
def submit():
    # Handle form submission
    return "Form submitted"

if __name__ == '__main__':
    app.run(debug=True)
```

Implementing CSRF Protection in Django

Django includes **CSRF protection** by default, which can be enabled by ensuring that the middleware is set in settings.py:

1. **Ensure CSRF Middleware is Enabled**:

```python
python
```

```python
MIDDLEWARE = [
```

```
'django.middleware.csrf.CsrfViewMiddlewar
e',
    # Other middleware...
]
```

2. **Using CSRF Token in Templates**:

In Django templates, include the `{% csrf_token %}`
tag inside form elements to add the CSRF token to form
submissions:

html

```
<form method="POST">
    {% csrf_token %}
    <input type="text" name="data">
    <button type="submit">Submit</button>
</form>
```

18.3 OAuth and OpenID Connect

OAuth2 and **OpenID Connect** (OIDC) are two widely used
authentication protocols that allow for secure API access. OAuth2
is used for authorization, while OpenID Connect extends OAuth2
for **authentication**.

1. OAuth2 (Authorization)

OAuth2 allows users to grant third-party applications access to their resources without sharing their credentials. OAuth2 uses **access tokens** to grant limited access to the user's data.

- **Authorization Code Flow**: The most common OAuth2 flow, where the user is redirected to the authorization server to log in and then returns with an authorization code. This code is exchanged for an access token.
- **Implicit Flow**: Suitable for client-side applications (e.g., single-page apps), where the access token is returned directly without an intermediate authorization code.
- **Client Credentials Flow**: Used for server-to-server communication where the client is acting on its own behalf.

Implementing OAuth2 with Flask

You can use **Flask-OAuthlib** to implement OAuth2 in a Flask application:

1. **Install Flask-OAuthlib**:

bash

```
pip install Flask-OAuthlib
```

2. **Configure OAuth2 Provider**:

```python
python

from flask import Flask, redirect, url_for
from     flask_oauthlib.provider     import
OAuth2Provider

app = Flask(__name__)
oauth = OAuth2Provider(app)

@app.route('/login')
def login():
    return 'Login Page'

if __name__ == '__main__':
    app.run(debug=True)
```

2. OpenID Connect (Authentication)

OpenID Connect is an identity layer built on top of OAuth2 that allows applications to authenticate users and obtain their profile information.

- **OIDC Flow**: Similar to OAuth2, but with the added benefit of obtaining user identity information (such as email, profile name) by requesting an **ID token**.

Implementing OpenID Connect in Django

To implement OIDC in Django, you can use the **django-allauth** library, which supports authentication via OAuth2 and OpenID Connect.

1. **Install django-allauth**:

   bash

   ```
   pip install django-allauth
   ```

2. **Configure OIDC** in `settings.py`:

   python

   ```
   INSTALLED_APPS = [
       'allauth',
       'allauth.account',
       'allauth.socialaccount',

   'allauth.socialaccount.providers.oauth2',
   ]
   ```

3. **Set Up OAuth2 Providers** (e.g., Google, Facebook) in your Django Admin.

Summary of Key Concepts

In this chapter, we:

- Discussed **security best practices** for securing APIs, including HTTPS, strong authentication, and input validation.
- Explained how to protect against **CORS (Cross-Origin Resource Sharing)** and **CSRF (Cross-Site Request Forgery)** attacks in both **Flask** and **Django**.
- Explored how to implement **OAuth2** and **OpenID Connect** for securing API access and handling authentication and authorization.

Securing your API is a critical part of building reliable, trustworthy services. By following best practices and implementing proper authentication, authorization, and protection mechanisms, you can safeguard your API from common vulnerabilities and attacks. In the next chapters, we'll explore more advanced topics like logging, monitoring, and scaling APIs.

CHAPTER 19

BUILDING AN API WITH FLASK MICROSERVICES

Microservices is an architectural style where an application is structured as a collection of loosely coupled, independently deployable services. Each service is responsible for a specific business function and communicates with other services through well-defined APIs, often using protocols like **HTTP** or **message queues**.

In this chapter, we will explore **microservices**, how to build **microservices with Flask**, and how different services can communicate with each other using **REST** and **message brokers** like **RabbitMQ**.

19.1 What Are Microservices?

Microservices Overview

Microservices are an approach to software architecture where the application is broken down into smaller, modular, and independent services, each responsible for a specific task or domain within the business. Unlike traditional **monolithic** architectures, where all functions of the application are tightly integrated into a single codebase, microservices offer more flexibility and scalability.

Key Characteristics of Microservices:

- **Single Responsibility**: Each microservice handles a specific function or domain, such as user management, payment processing, or product inventory.
- **Independently Deployable**: Microservices can be deployed and updated independently of each other. This allows teams to release new features or updates for specific services without affecting the entire system.
- **Technology Agnostic**: Each microservice can be built using different technologies, allowing teams to use the best tools for the job.
- **Communication**: Microservices communicate with each other through well-defined APIs, typically using REST, HTTP, or message brokers like RabbitMQ or Kafka.
- **Scalability**: Since each service is independent, it can be scaled independently based on its specific requirements.

Benefits of Microservices:

1. **Modularity**: Microservices provide clear boundaries for different parts of an application, making it easier to manage and scale individual components.

2. **Resilience**: If one microservice fails, the others continue to function, allowing the system to remain operational.

3. **Flexibility**: Microservices allow you to use different programming languages, databases, or frameworks for different services, making it easier to experiment and adopt new technologies.

4. **Faster Development**: Teams can work independently on different microservices, speeding up development cycles and allowing faster releases.

5. **Easier Scaling**: You can scale individual services based on demand, optimizing resource usage.

19.2 Building Microservices with Flask

Flask is a popular web framework for Python that's lightweight and easy to use. It's an excellent choice for building microservices due to its minimalistic design and flexibility. Let's go through the steps of breaking a monolithic API into microservices using Flask.

Step 1: Identifying Services

Before you begin, identify the different business functions that can be separated into individual services. For example:

- **User Service**: Handles user authentication, profile management, etc.

- **Product Service**: Manages product information, prices, inventory, etc.

- **Order Service**: Handles customer orders, payments, shipping, etc.

Step 2: Creating Flask Microservices

Let's build two simple microservices using Flask. One will be a **User Service**, and the other will be a **Product Service**.

1. **User Service**: A simple API that returns user details.

   app_user.py (User Service):

```python
python

from flask import Flask, jsonify

app = Flask(__name__)

# Dummy user data
users = {
    1: {'name': 'John Doe', 'email':
'john@example.com'},
    2: {'name': 'Jane Smith', 'email':
'jane@example.com'}
}
```

```
@app.route('/users/<int:user_id>',
methods=['GET'])
def get_user(user_id):
    user = users.get(user_id)
    if user:
        return jsonify(user)
    return jsonify({'error': 'User not
found'}), 404


if __name__ == '__main__':
    app.run(port=5001, debug=True)
```

This service will listen on port **5001** and serve user data based on user IDs.

2. **Product Service**: A simple API that returns product details.

    app_product.py (Product Service):

```python

from flask import Flask, jsonify

app = Flask(__name__)

# Dummy product data
products = {
    101: {'name': 'Laptop', 'price':
1000},
```

230

```
      102:  {'name':  'Smartphone',  'price':
500}
}


@app.route('/products/<int:product_id>',
methods=['GET'])
def get_product(product_id):
    product = products.get(product_id)
    if product:
        return jsonify(product)
    return jsonify({'error':  'Product  not
found'}),  404


if __name__ == '__main__':
    app.run(port=5002, debug=True)
```

This service will listen on port **5002** and serve product data based on product IDs.

Step 3: Running the Microservices

To run the microservices:

1. Start the **User Service**:

```bash
bash
```

```
python app_user.py
```

The User Service will be accessible at `http://localhost:5001/users/{user_id}`.

2. Start the **Product Service**:

```bash
python app_product.py
```

The Product Service will be accessible at `http://localhost:5002/products/{product_id}`.

You now have two separate microservices running, each responsible for a specific domain.

Step 4: API Gateway (Optional)

In a production environment, you might want to use an **API Gateway** to route requests to the appropriate microservices based on the request path. This can be done using tools like **Kong**, **Nginx**, or **AWS API Gateway**.

For now, you can manually test both microservices by accessing them through their respective endpoints.

19.3 Inter-Service Communication

Microservices need to communicate with each other. There are two common methods for communication between services:

- **RESTful APIs** (HTTP-based communication).
- **Message Brokers** (e.g., **RabbitMQ** or **Kafka**) for asynchronous communication.

1. RESTful APIs for Communication

In our Flask microservices, communication between services can be achieved using **HTTP requests**. For example, the **Order Service** could communicate with the **User Service** and **Product Service** to retrieve data when processing an order.

Here's an example where the **Order Service** makes an HTTP request to the **User Service**:

python

```
import requests

USER_SERVICE_URL                              =
"http://localhost:5001/users/1"
PRODUCT_SERVICE_URL                           =
"http://localhost:5002/products/101"

def get_order_details():
```

```
    user_response                        =
requests.get(USER_SERVICE_URL)
    product_response                     =
requests.get(PRODUCT_SERVICE_URL)

    if   user_response.status_code   ==   200   and
product_response.status_code == 200:
        user_data = user_response.json()
        product_data = product_response.json()

        return {
            'user': user_data,
            'product': product_data
        }
    else:
        return {'error': 'Data not found'}

# Simulating an order request
order_details = get_order_details()
print(order_details)
```

In this example, the **Order Service** fetches data from both the **User Service** and the **Product Service** using HTTP GET requests.

2. Using Message Brokers (RabbitMQ)

For more complex microservice architectures, asynchronous communication using a **message broker** like **RabbitMQ** is preferred. This decouples services and allows them to

234

communicate asynchronously, making it easier to handle high volumes of requests.

1. **Install RabbitMQ**: You can install **RabbitMQ** on your local machine or use a cloud service.

2. **Integrating RabbitMQ in Flask**: You can use **Celery** for task queueing in Flask and integrate it with RabbitMQ for communication between services.

```bash
pip install celery[redis]
```

3. **Setting Up Celery with Flask**: Here's a simplified example of how to use **Celery** with Flask and **RabbitMQ** for inter-service communication. Celery allows you to queue tasks that are processed asynchronously.

app_celery.py (For managing tasks):

```python
from celery import Celery

app         =         Celery('tasks',
broker='pyamqp://guest@localhost//')

@app.task
def process_order(user_id, product_id):
```

235

```
# Simulate order processing
return    f"Order    processed    for    user
{user_id} and product {product_id}"
```

With this setup, the Flask app can send tasks to the message broker, which will be handled asynchronously.

Summary of Key Concepts

In this chapter, we:

- Explored the concept of **microservices**, understanding their benefits such as modularity, scalability, and resilience.
- Built two simple **Flask microservices**: one for managing users and the other for managing products, each handling a specific business domain.
- Implemented **RESTful communication** between services using HTTP requests.
- Introduced the concept of **message brokers**, like **RabbitMQ**, for asynchronous communication between microservices, providing decoupling and improved scalability.

Microservices allow you to build scalable and maintainable applications by breaking down monolithic architectures into smaller, independently deployable services. In the next chapters, we will explore advanced microservice topics such as service discovery, API Gateway, and deploying microservices in production.

CHAPTER 20

BUILDING AN API WITH DJANGO MICROSERVICES

In this chapter, we will explore how to implement **microservices** using **Django**, a robust web framework for building APIs. We will cover how to structure Django applications in a microservice architecture and demonstrate how to manage communication between microservices, allowing them to work together efficiently.

20.1 Implementing Microservices with Django

What is a Microservice in Django?

A **microservice architecture** in Django involves breaking a monolithic application into smaller, independently deployable services. Each service is responsible for a specific business domain, such as **user management**, **product management**, or **order processing**. Each microservice typically has its own **database** and communicates with other microservices via APIs, most commonly through **RESTful APIs**.

How to Apply the Microservices Architecture Using Django

1. **Define Boundaries for Microservices**: The first step in building microservices with Django is to define the boundaries of each microservice. For instance:

    o **User Service**: Handles user authentication, user profiles, and permissions.

    o **Product Service**: Manages products, prices, and inventory.

    o **Order Service**: Handles customer orders, payments, and order status.

2. **Set Up Separate Django Projects for Each Service**: Each microservice will be a separate Django project. This allows each service to be developed, deployed, and scaled independently. You can create a new Django project for each service, such as:

bash

```
django-admin startproject users_service
django-admin startproject products_service
django-admin startproject orders_service
```

These separate services will each have their own set of models, views, and databases. This separation of concerns is the core of microservices.

3. **Use Django Rest Framework (DRF) for API Endpoints**: For each microservice, Django Rest Framework (DRF) is an excellent choice to create **RESTful APIs**. You can define API views for each service and expose endpoints that other services can consume.

Example: **User Service** (`users_service/views.py`)

python

```
from rest_framework.views import APIView
from rest_framework.response import Response
from rest_framework import status

class UserAPIView(APIView):
    def get(self, request, user_id):
        # Simulate fetching user data
        user_data = {'id': user_id,
'name': 'John Doe', 'email':
'john@example.com'}
        return Response(user_data,
status=status.HTTP_200_OK)
```

In this example, we define an endpoint `/users/{user_id}` to retrieve user data.

240

4. **Use Docker for Containerization** (Optional but recommended for production): Since microservices are independently deployable, using **Docker** to containerize each service is a common practice. This ensures that each microservice is isolated, making it easier to deploy and scale.

Docker Example: A basic `Dockerfile` for a Django service.

```
Dockerfile

FROM python:3.9

WORKDIR /app

 requirements.txt .
RUN pip install -r requirements.txt

   .  .

EXPOSE 8000
CMD ["python", "manage.py", "runserver", "0.0.0.0:8000"]
```

Each microservice can have its own Docker container, which can be run in isolation or managed using **Docker Compose**.

241

5. **Use a Centralized Database or Separate Databases for Each Service?**

In a microservices architecture, each service typically has its own **database** to maintain loose coupling between services. However, if there's a need for sharing data, you can use **event-driven** architectures or **API communication** to fetch data from other services when needed.

20.2 Inter-API Communication in Django

Once you've broken your application into microservices, you'll need a way for these services to communicate with each other. Django microservices typically communicate via **RESTful APIs**, but you can also use asynchronous messaging with message brokers (like **RabbitMQ** or **Kafka**) for event-driven communication.

1. RESTful Communication Between Services

The simplest way for Django microservices to communicate is through **REST APIs**. A microservice can make HTTP requests to another microservice's API to access or modify data.

For example, the **Order Service** might need to retrieve product details from the **Product Service** when an order is placed. The

242

Order Service can make an HTTP GET request to the **Product Service** to fetch product details.

Example: Order Service Communicating with Product Service

python

```
import requests

PRODUCT_SERVICE_URL         =      "http://product-
service:8000/products/{product_id}"

def get_product_data(product_id):
    response                                =
requests.get(PRODUCT_SERVICE_URL.format(product
_id=product_id))
    if response.status_code == 200:
        return response.json()
    return {'error': 'Product not found'}

# Example usage in an order endpoint
def create_order(request):
    product_id = request.data['product_id']
    product_data = get_product_data(product_id)
    if 'error' in product_data:
        return Response({'error': 'Product not
available'}, status=404)
    # Process order logic...
```

243

```
    return        Response({'message':        'Order
created'}, status=201)
```

In this example:

- The **Order Service** makes an HTTP request to the **Product Service** to fetch product data.
- If the product exists, the order is processed; if not, an error response is returned.

2. Using Message Brokers (RabbitMQ) for Asynchronous Communication

For more complex communication, especially when you want to decouple services or handle asynchronous workflows, you can use a **message broker** like **RabbitMQ** or **Kafka**. This is useful for event-driven architectures, where services communicate by sending messages to a message queue that other services can consume.

Example: Using RabbitMQ with Django

1. **Install Celery and Celery-RabbitMQ:**

    bash

```
pip install celery
pip install celery[redis]
pip install django-celery-results
```

2. **Configure Celery for Django**: In your Django project (`settings.py`), configure Celery to use RabbitMQ as the broker.

python

```python
# settings.py
CELERY_BROKER_URL                              =
'pyamqp://guest@localhost//'
CELERY_RESULT_BACKEND = 'django-db'
```

3. **Create a Celery Task**:

   tasks.py (In your service app):

   python

```python
from celery import shared_task
import requests

@shared_task
def process_order(product_id):
    # Fetch product data asynchronously
    response                                   =
requests.get(f"http://product-
service:8000/products/{product_id}")
    if response.status_code == 200:
        product_data = response.json()
        # Process the order
```

245

```
        return   f"Order   processed   for
{product_data['name']}"
    return "Product not found"
```

4. **Call Celery Task**:

In your Django view, call the Celery task to handle asynchronous processing.

python

```python
from .tasks import process_order

def create_order(request):
    product_id                           =
request.data['product_id']
    process_order.delay(product_id)      #
Call asynchronously
    return Response({"message": "Order is
being processed"}, status=202)
```

5. **Run Celery Worker**: To process tasks, run the Celery worker in the terminal:

bash

```bash
celery  -A  your_project_name  worker  --
loglevel=info
```

In this example, the **Order Service** will create orders asynchronously by queuing tasks in RabbitMQ, and another service (Celery worker) will consume those tasks and process the orders.

20.3 Managing Data Flow Between Microservices in Django

Managing data flow in a microservices architecture can be challenging, especially when you need to synchronize data between services or when one service needs to access data from another. Here are some common patterns for handling inter-service communication:

1. Synchronous Communication via REST

This is the simplest form of communication, where one service calls another via REST APIs. This is suitable when the response time is critical, and you need the data immediately.

2. Asynchronous Communication with Event-Driven Architecture

Using a message broker like **RabbitMQ** or **Kafka**, services can communicate asynchronously. This is ideal for handling tasks that don't require immediate feedback, like **order processing**, **email notifications**, or **logging**.

3. Database Replication (Optional)

In some cases, you might need to replicate data across microservices. For example, the **Product Service** might need to share inventory data with the **Order Service**. You can achieve this by replicating certain data across services using asynchronous message queues or using **database replication** techniques.

4. API Gateway for Routing Requests

An **API Gateway** can be used to route requests to the appropriate microservice based on the endpoint. It acts as a reverse proxy that aggregates responses from multiple services, improving scalability and security.

Summary of Key Concepts

In this chapter, we:

- **Explored the concept of microservices** and how to structure Django applications as a collection of independent, loosely coupled services.
- **Built microservices with Django**, creating multiple services for user, product, and order management using Django Rest Framework (DRF) for API creation.

- **Demonstrated communication between microservices** using **RESTful APIs** for synchronous communication and **message brokers (RabbitMQ)** for asynchronous communication.

- Discussed patterns for **managing data flow between services**, including **synchronous REST communication**, **asynchronous event-driven architectures**, and **using an API Gateway** for routing requests.

By building Django microservices, you can create scalable, resilient, and maintainable applications that can evolve independently. In the next chapters, we will delve into best practices for deploying and monitoring microservices in production environments.

CHAPTER 21

ASYNCHRONOUS TASKS AND BACKGROUND JOBS

In modern applications, especially APIs, there are often tasks that can take a long time to complete, such as sending emails, processing images, or querying large datasets. These tasks, if run synchronously, would block the entire application and degrade performance. To avoid this, we use **asynchronous tasks** and **background jobs** to handle long-running processes outside the normal request-response cycle. In this chapter, we will cover how to handle asynchronous tasks in **Flask** using **Celery** and explore **async views** in **Django**.

21.1 Why Asynchronous Tasks Are Important

Handling Long-Running Tasks Without Blocking

Asynchronous tasks allow your application to process long-running operations without blocking the main thread that handles incoming API requests. Without asynchronous handling, these long-running tasks would slow down your API's responsiveness. This is especially problematic for user-facing applications where users expect fast responses.

Example Scenario:

- **Sending emails**: Sending confirmation emails or notifications often involves connecting to external services. This can take time, and if done synchronously, it will delay the response to the user.
- **Processing data**: Tasks such as image processing, video transcoding, or complex data analysis may take a significant amount of time to complete. If these tasks block the main API thread, the application becomes unresponsive.
- **Third-party API calls**: External services, like payment gateways or social media integrations, may have slow response times. Making synchronous calls to these services can delay the user's request.

By offloading these tasks to background workers, the application remains responsive, and the tasks are handled asynchronously.

Benefits of Asynchronous Tasks:

- **Improved user experience**: Users get immediate responses from your API while background tasks run.
- **Better resource utilization**: Asynchronous tasks run independently, allowing your API to handle other incoming requests.

- **Scalability**: Background jobs can be distributed across multiple workers to scale with the application's needs.

21.2 Using Celery with Flask

Celery is a powerful and flexible distributed task queue system that can handle background jobs. It allows you to offload long-running tasks to separate workers, making it ideal for Flask applications that need to handle asynchronous operations.

Setting Up Celery with Flask

1. **Install Celery and Redis**: Celery requires a message broker like **Redis** or **RabbitMQ** to queue tasks. In this example, we'll use **Redis**.

   Install the necessary dependencies:

   bash

   ```
   pip install celery redis flask
   ```

2. **Create Flask App with Celery Integration**:

   app.py (Flask App with Celery):

   python

```python
from flask import Flask
from celery import Celery
from time import sleep

# Flask app setup
app = Flask(__name__)
app.config['SECRET_KEY']                =
'your_secret_key'

# Celery setup
def make_celery(app):
    celery = Celery(
        app.import_name,

backend=app.config['CELERY_RESULT_BACKEND
'],

broker=app.config['CELERY_BROKER_URL']
    )
    celery.conf.update(app.config)
    return celery

app.config.update(

CELERY_BROKER_URL='redis://localhost:6379
/0',

CELERY_RESULT_BACKEND='redis://localhost:
6379/0'
```

```
)

celery = make_celery(app)

# Define an asynchronous task
@celery.task
def long_task():
    sleep(10)   # Simulate a long-running task
    return "Task Completed!"

# Route to trigger the task
@app.route('/start_task')
def start_task():
    task = long_task.apply_async()  # Start the background task
    return f"Task started with task ID {task.id}"

if __name__ == '__main__':
    app.run(debug=True)
```

3. **Running Celery Worker**: After setting up Celery in your Flask app, you need to run a separate worker to handle the background tasks.

Start the Celery worker in a new terminal window:

```bash
bash
```

```
celery    -A    app.celery    worker    --
loglevel=info
```

4. **Testing**: To test the Flask app, start the Flask server:

```bash
bash
```

```
python app.py
```

Visit `http://localhost:5000/start_task` to trigger the background job. The task will run in the background without blocking the Flask API response.

21.3 Async Views in Django

In **Django**, asynchronous support has been introduced in **Django 3.1**, allowing views to be asynchronous and enabling Django to handle long-running tasks without blocking the server. Django now supports **asynchronous views** and can handle **async I/O operations** such as database queries or external API calls.

Setting Up Async Views in Django

To use async views in Django, you need to define your views as asynchronous by adding `async def` instead of `def`. Django will then handle the request asynchronously, allowing you to perform long-running tasks without blocking the main thread.

1. **Define an Asynchronous View in Django**:

views.py:

```python
python
```

```python
from django.http import JsonResponse
import asyncio

# Asynchronous view
async def async_view(request):
    await asyncio.sleep(5)   # Simulate a
long-running task
    return JsonResponse({"message": "Task
completed asynchronously!"})
```

2. **Configure URLs**: In urls.py, link to the async view:

urls.py:

```python
python
```

```python
from django.urls import path
from . import views

urlpatterns = [
    path('async_task/', views.async_view,
name='async_task'),
    ]
```

3. **Run the Django Server**: Start the Django development server with:

```bash
```

```
python manage.py runserver
```

4. **Testing**: When you visit `http://localhost:8000/async_task/`, the server will handle the request asynchronously and simulate a long-running task (such as database queries, external API calls, or complex computations) without blocking the response to the user.

Benefits of Async Views in Django:

- **Non-blocking I/O**: Async views allow Django to handle I/O-bound tasks (like API calls or database queries) asynchronously, improving overall performance.
- **Concurrency**: Django can handle multiple requests concurrently, which can improve the server's ability to handle high traffic loads.
- **Better user experience**: Async views allow long-running operations (e.g., sending emails or processing data) to run without keeping the user waiting.

Handling Asynchronous Tasks in Django with Celery

For background tasks in Django, **Celery** can be used in conjunction with Django's asynchronous views. This allows you to offload long-running tasks like image processing, sending emails, or generating reports.

1. **Set Up Celery in Django**:

   Install Celery and Redis:

   bash

   ```
   pip install celery redis
   ```

   In your Django project, create a new file called **celery.py** in the project root directory:

   celery.py:

   python

   ```
   from __future__ import absolute_import,
   unicode_literals
   import os
   from celery import Celery

   os.environ.setdefault('DJANGO_SETTINGS_MO
   DULE', 'your_project_name.settings')
   ```

```
app = Celery('your_project_name')

# Using a string here means the worker
doesn't have to serialize
# the configuration object to child
processes.
# - namespace='CELERY' means all celery-
related config keys should have a `CELERY_`
prefix.
app.config_from_object('django.conf:setti
ngs', namespace='CELERY')

# Load task modules from all registered
Django app configs.
app.autodiscover_tasks()
```

2. **Add Celery Settings to Django `settings.py`:**

settings.py:

python

```
CELERY_BROKER_URL                        =
'redis://localhost:6379/0'
CELERY_RESULT_BACKEND                    =
'redis://localhost:6379/0'
```

3. **Define a Celery Task**: In **tasks.py** of your Django app:

259

tasks.py:

```python
from celery import shared_task
import time

@shared_task
def long_running_task():
    time.sleep(10)
    return "Task Completed!"
```

4. **Call Celery Task**: In your Django view, you can call this background task using the `delay()` method:

views.py:

```python
from django.http import JsonResponse
from .tasks import long_running_task

def start_task(request):
    long_running_task.delay()  # Run in the background
    return JsonResponse({"message": "Task started!"})
```

5. **Run Celery Worker**: In the terminal, run the Celery worker:

```bash
bash
```

```
celery -A your_project_name worker --
loglevel=info
```

6. **Testing**: Now, when you visit `http://localhost:8000/start_task/`, the task will run in the background while the user receives an immediate response.

Summary of Key Concepts

In this chapter, we:

- **Discussed the importance of asynchronous tasks** and background jobs for handling long-running processes without blocking API responses, improving user experience and performance.
- **Set up Celery in Flask** to handle background tasks and run them asynchronously, allowing Flask to stay responsive to user requests.
- **Explored async views in Django**, which allow the application to handle long-running tasks asynchronously and improve concurrency.

261

- **Integrated Celery with Django** to offload tasks like sending emails or processing data into background jobs, improving performance and scalability.

Asynchronous tasks and background job processing are essential for building scalable, efficient applications, and they enable better handling of tasks that would otherwise block the user experience. In the next chapters, we will cover advanced techniques like logging, monitoring, and deploying these systems.

CHAPTER 22

MONITORING AND LOGGING YOUR API

Monitoring and logging are vital aspects of maintaining and improving the performance, reliability, and security of your APIs. By monitoring the health of your API and tracking key metrics, you can identify issues early, optimize performance, and provide a better experience for users. Logging, on the other hand, helps you troubleshoot problems, track requests, and understand application behavior.

In this chapter, we'll explore why monitoring is crucial, how to implement logging in **Flask**, and how to use **Django** tools and third-party services for monitoring the health and performance of your API.

22.1 Why Monitoring is Crucial

Understanding the Importance of Monitoring

Monitoring your API allows you to gain real-time insights into its health and performance. Without monitoring, it's challenging to detect issues such as slow response times, failed requests, or security breaches before they affect your users. Here are the key reasons why monitoring is critical:

- **Performance Optimization**: Monitoring helps track response times, server load, and database queries, providing insights into bottlenecks that can be addressed to improve performance.
- **User Experience**: By continuously monitoring the API, you can identify when something goes wrong, such as slow endpoints or high error rates, and take corrective action before users are impacted.
- **Proactive Issue Resolution**: With proper monitoring in place, you can receive alerts when an issue arises (e.g., a spike in errors), allowing you to fix problems before they become critical.
- **Security**: Monitoring also plays a key role in detecting potential security breaches, such as suspicious activity or unauthorized access attempts.
- **Compliance and Auditing**: If your API is used for financial, medical, or other regulated industries, monitoring and logging are essential for maintaining compliance and auditing activities.

Key Metrics to Monitor in APIs

- **Response Time**: Measure the time it takes for your API to respond to requests. Slow response times could indicate performance issues.
- **Error Rates**: Track the number of failed requests (e.g., HTTP 500 errors). A high error rate can indicate that something is wrong.
- **Request Volume**: Monitor the number of requests your API is handling. This helps ensure that your infrastructure can handle high traffic loads.
- **Uptime**: Measure the availability of your API to ensure it's up and running. Downtime can cause significant disruption to users.
- **Latency**: Track the delay between sending a request and receiving a response. High latency can lead to poor user experience.

22.2 Logging with Flask

Logging is essential for troubleshooting, monitoring, and debugging your application. Flask provides built-in support for logging, allowing you to log events such as incoming requests, errors, and custom messages.

Setting Up Logging in Flask

To configure logging in Flask, you can use Python's **logging module**.

1. **Basic Setup for Flask Logging**:

   Add the following to your `app.py` (or main Flask application file):

   python

```python
import logging
from flask import Flask, jsonify

app = Flask(__name__)

# Set up logging
logging.basicConfig(level=logging.DEBUG,
format='%(asctime)s  -  %(levelname)s  -
%(message)s')

@app.route('/')
def home():
    app.logger.info("Home   endpoint   was
accessed.")
    return jsonify(message="Welcome to the
API!")
```

266

```
@app.route('/error')
def error():
    app.logger.error("An    error    occurred
while accessing the error endpoint.")
    return jsonify(message="Something went
wrong"), 500

if __name__ == '__main__':
    app.run(debug=True)
```

Explanation:

- o **logging.basicConfig()**: Configures the logging system, setting the log level to DEBUG (which means it will log all messages of level DEBUG and higher) and specifying the log format.
- o **app.logger.info()** and **app.logger.error()**: Log messages of different severity levels (info and error).

2. **Log to a File**: You can configure Flask to write logs to a file instead of printing them to the console.

python

```
handler = logging.FileHandler('app.log')
handler.setLevel(logging.DEBUG)
app.logger.addHandler(handler)
```

With this configuration, logs will be written to a file named `app.log`.

3. **Logging Request and Response Data**: You can log the details of incoming requests and outgoing responses, such as headers and payloads, to track API usage and troubleshoot issues.

python

```
@app.before_request
def log_request():
    app.logger.info(f"Incoming       request:
{request.method} {request.url}")

@app.after_request
def log_response(response):
    app.logger.info(f"Outgoing       response:
{response.status}")
    return response
```

Best Practices for Flask Logging

- **Use Different Log Levels**: Use DEBUG, INFO, WARNING, ERROR, and CRITICAL log levels to categorize the severity of messages.
- **Avoid Logging Sensitive Data**: Be careful not to log sensitive information (e.g., passwords, credit card numbers).

- **Log to External Services**: For production applications, consider logging to external services like **Loggly**, **Sentry**, or **Datadog** for better aggregation and analysis.

22.3 Monitoring with Django

Django has several built-in tools and integrations for monitoring the performance and health of your API. Additionally, there are third-party services and tools that can help you monitor Django applications effectively.

Using Django Tools for Monitoring

1. **Django Debug Toolbar**: The **Django Debug Toolbar** is a powerful tool for debugging and monitoring your Django application. It provides detailed information about each request, including the time taken, SQL queries executed, and more.

   Install Django Debug Toolbar:

   bash

   ```
   pip install django-debug-toolbar
   ```

   Configure in `settings.py`:

   python

```
INSTALLED_APPS = [
    # Other apps...
    'debug_toolbar',
]

MIDDLEWARE = [
    # Other middleware...

'debug_toolbar.middleware.DebugToolbarMid
dleware',
]

INTERNAL_IPS = ['127.0.0.1']   # Make sure
it only shows on local requests
```

The debug toolbar will appear on your local development server, showing real-time performance data, SQL queries, cache usage, and more.

2. **Django Logging**: Django has built-in support for logging, similar to Flask. You can configure logging in the `settings.py` file.

    Configure Logging in `settings.py`:

    ```
    python

    LOGGING = {
    ```

```
'version': 1,
'disable_existing_loggers': False,
'handlers': {
    'file': {
        'level': 'DEBUG',
        'class':
'logging.FileHandler',
        'filename': 'django_app.log',
    },
},
'loggers': {
    'django': {
        'handlers': ['file'],
        'level': 'DEBUG',
        'propagate': True,
    },
},
}
```

This configuration writes logs to a file (django_app.log). You can modify this to log to a console or external service if needed.

3. **Monitoring with Third-Party Tools**:

To monitor the health of your Django application and get real-time insights, you can integrate third-party tools like:

o **Sentry**: An error-tracking tool that helps capture and monitor exceptions in your Django application.

o **Datadog**: A full-service monitoring tool that integrates with Django to track API health, uptime, and performance metrics.

o **New Relic**: Provides application performance monitoring (APM) and real-time metrics for Django apps.

Example: Integrating Sentry with Django:

4. **Install Sentry**:

bash

```
pip install sentry-sdk
```

5. **Configure Sentry in `settings.py`**:

python

```
import sentry_sdk
from sentry_sdk.integrations.django
import DjangoIntegration

sentry_sdk.init(
    dsn="https://your-dsn-
url.sentry.io/your-project-id",
```

```
integrations=[DjangoIntegration()]
)
```

With this integration, any errors or exceptions in your Django app will be automatically reported to Sentry, where you can monitor and resolve issues.

Real-Time API Monitoring with Prometheus and Grafana:

For advanced monitoring, you can integrate **Prometheus** (an open-source monitoring tool) with **Grafana** (a data visualization tool) to track metrics like response times, error rates, and traffic volume.

1. **Install Prometheus Client**:

```bash
pip install prometheus_client
```

2. **Add Prometheus Middleware** in Django:

```python
from      prometheus_client      import
make_wsgi_app
from  prometheus_client.exposition  import
basic_auth_handler
```

273

```
from django.http import HttpResponse
from django.conf import settings


def metrics_view(request):
    return HttpResponse(make_wsgi_app())
```

3. **Set Up Grafana** to visualize metrics from Prometheus.

Summary of Key Concepts

In this chapter, we:

- Discussed the importance of **monitoring and logging** to track API performance, identify issues, and improve the overall user experience.
- Explored **logging in Flask**, including setting up basic logging and writing logs to files, as well as using **Flask logging** for real-time debugging and analysis.
- Demonstrated how to monitor APIs in **Django** using built-in tools like the **Django Debug Toolbar** and **Django Logging**, and how to integrate third-party services like **Sentry**, **Datadog**, and **Prometheus** for advanced monitoring and error tracking.

By implementing effective monitoring and logging, you can improve the reliability, performance, and security of your APIs,

274

providing better insights into how your application is functioning and where improvements are needed. In the next chapters, we will explore additional best practices for scaling and securing your APIs.

CHAPTER 23

BUILDING A DOCUMENTATION SYSTEM FOR YOUR API

A well-documented API is crucial for developers, stakeholders, and users to understand how to interact with your service. It helps developers integrate your API seamlessly into their applications, reduces the chance of errors, and improves the overall user experience. In this chapter, we will cover why API documentation is important, how to use **Swagger/OpenAPI** for documentation, and demonstrate how to integrate API documentation in both **Flask** and **Django**.

23.1 Why API Documentation is Important

The Role of API Documentation

API documentation serves as a blueprint for developers to understand the endpoints, data models, methods, parameters, and expected responses of an API. Without proper documentation, even the most well-built APIs can lead to confusion, misuse, and errors.

Real-World Examples of Poorly Documented APIs

1. **Facebook Graph API**: In its early days, the **Facebook Graph API** was heavily criticized for being poorly documented. This lack of clarity led to a slow adoption rate, bugs in third-party applications, and ultimately, frustrations for developers trying to integrate Facebook into their apps.

2. **Twitter API**: Similarly, the **Twitter API** underwent several versions, and as the API evolved, documentation issues arose. Developers struggled to keep up with changes, and certain parts of the API were often left under-explained, leading to frequent errors and misunderstandings.

3. **Custom Internal APIs**: Many internal APIs in organizations are either not documented or poorly documented. When new developers join the team or when the API is handed off to other teams, they often face confusion about its usage, endpoints, and expected behaviors. This slows down development and creates an unnecessary learning curve.

Consequences of Poor API Documentation:

- **Increased Development Time**: Developers waste time understanding how the API works.

- **Increased Error Rate**: Lack of clarity often leads to incorrect API usage, leading to errors in the system.
- **Frustration**: Poor documentation can lead to frustration among developers, reducing adoption of the API.
- **Inability to Scale**: As APIs grow, their complexity increases. Without comprehensive documentation, scaling the API becomes harder.

Good API documentation improves clarity, reduces errors, and allows teams to focus on building features instead of figuring out how to use the API.

23.2 Using Swagger/OpenAPI for Documentation

Swagger (now known as **OpenAPI**) is a specification for describing RESTful APIs. With Swagger, you can easily create, visualize, and maintain API documentation. **Swagger UI** provides an interactive interface that allows users to try out API calls directly from the documentation.

Why Use Swagger/OpenAPI?

- **Standardization**: OpenAPI is widely adopted, making it a standard for API documentation.

- **Interactive Documentation**: Swagger UI allows users to make API calls directly from the documentation, streamlining the testing process.
- **Automatic Generation**: With the right tools, you can auto-generate API documentation from your code, ensuring consistency between implementation and documentation.

Swagger/OpenAPI Benefits:

- **Interactive UI**: Developers can interact with your API directly from the documentation, testing endpoints, parameters, and responses.
- **Code First**: Generate documentation from code annotations, ensuring up-to-date docs.
- **Integration with API Clients**: Clients can generate SDKs and API clients automatically based on the OpenAPI specification.

23.3 Documenting Your Flask API

In Flask, you can integrate **Swagger/OpenAPI** documentation using the **Flask-RESTful** extension in combination with **Flask-Swagger-UI** or **Flask-Swagger-Doc**. This allows you to easily create RESTful APIs and automatically generate Swagger documentation.

279

Integrating Swagger with Flask-RESTful

1. **Install Required Packages**:

   bash

   ```bash
   pip install flask flask-restful flask-swagger-ui
   ```

2. **Create Flask App with Swagger UI**:

   Here's a simple Flask app with **Swagger UI**:

   app.py:

   python

   ```python
   from flask import Flask, jsonify
   from flask_restful import Api, Resource
   from flask_swagger_ui import get_swaggerui_blueprint

   app = Flask(__name__)
   api = Api(app)

   # API Documentation URL
   SWAGGER_URL = '/swagger'
   API_URL = '/static/swagger.json'

   # Swagger UI setup
   ```

```python
swagger_ui_blueprint                        =
get_swaggerui_blueprint(SWAGGER_URL,
API_URL, config={'app_name': "Flask API"})
app.register_blueprint(swagger_ui_bluepri
nt, url_prefix=SWAGGER_URL)

# Example Resource
class HelloWorld(Resource):
    def get(self):
        return jsonify({"message": "Hello,
World!"})

api.add_resource(HelloWorld, '/')

if __name__ == '__main__':
    app.run(debug=True)
```

3. **Swagger JSON Specification**: You'll need to create a `swagger.json` file that defines the API endpoints, parameters, and responses.

   swagger.json:

```json
json

{
  "swagger": "2.0",
  "info": {
    "title": "Flask API",
    "version": "1.0"
```

```
    },
  "paths": {
    "/": {
      "get": {
        "summary":    "Returns    a    hello
message",
        "responses": {
          "200": {
            "description":      "A      hello
message",
            "schema": {
              "type": "object",
              "properties": {
                "message": {
                  "type": "string"
                }
              }
            }
          }
        }
      }
    }
  }
}
```

4. **Run the Application**: When you visit http://localhost:5000/swagger, you'll see the **Swagger UI** documentation, which will allow you to interact with the API.

23.4 Documenting Your Django API

In Django, you can use **Django Rest Framework (DRF)** in combination with **drf-yasg** to auto-generate Swagger/OpenAPI documentation for your API.

Integrating Swagger with Django Rest Framework

1. **Install Required Packages**: First, install the necessary packages:

   bash

   ```bash
   pip install drf-yasg
   pip install djangorestframework
   ```

2. **Configure DRF and drf-yasg in `settings.py`**: Add `rest_framework` and `drf_yasg` to the `INSTALLED_APPS` in settings.py.

   settings.py:

   python

   ```python
   INSTALLED_APPS = [
       'rest_framework',
       'drf_yasg',
       # Other apps...
   ```

283

]

3. **Set Up Swagger Documentation**:

In your Django `urls.py`, configure `drf-yasg` to generate Swagger documentation automatically.

urls.py:

```python
from rest_framework.views import APIView
from rest_framework.response import Response
from rest_framework import status
from rest_framework import serializers
from rest_framework.decorators import api_view
from rest_framework import generics
from drf_yasg.views import get_schema_view
from drf_yasg import openapi

# Swagger setup
schema_view = get_schema_view(
    openapi.Info(
        title="Django API",
        default_version='v1',
        description="Test description",
```

```
terms_of_service="https://www.google.com/
policies/terms/",

contact=openapi.Contact(email="contact@dj
ango.local"),
        license=openapi.License(name="BSD
License"),
    ),
    public=True,
)

# Example DRF View
class HelloWorldView(APIView):
    def get(self, request):
        return          Response({"message":
"Hello, World!"})

urlpatterns = [
    path('hello/',
HelloWorldView.as_view(), name='hello'),
    path('swagger/',
schema_view.as_view(), name='swagger'),
]
```

4. **Run the Application**: When you visit
   `http://localhost:8000/swagger/`, you'll see the
   Swagger UI with auto-generated API documentation for
   all the endpoints in your Django application.

285

Summary of Key Concepts

In this chapter, we:

- **Explained the importance of API documentation** for developers and users, emphasizing the risks of poorly documented APIs.
- **Used Swagger/OpenAPI** to auto-generate interactive API documentation for both **Flask** and **Django** applications.
- **Demonstrated how to integrate Swagger with Flask** using **Flask-RESTful** and **Flask-Swagger-UI** for easy API documentation.
- **Implemented automatic API documentation in Django** using **DRF** and **drf-yasg**, allowing you to generate and visualize Swagger documentation directly from your Django API.

Well-documented APIs improve collaboration, reduce errors, and accelerate development. With tools like Swagger/OpenAPI, you can automate and maintain documentation for your APIs, ensuring they remain up-to-date as the API evolves. In the next chapters, we'll dive deeper into deploying APIs, versioning, and securing your API documentation.

286

CHAPTER 24

CONSUMING APIS WITH PYTHON (CLIENTS)

In this chapter, we will focus on consuming **RESTful APIs** using Python. Python provides several libraries that make it easy to interact with external services, one of the most popular being the **requests** library. We will cover how to make HTTP requests, handle API responses, parse data, and deal with common issues like checking status codes and handling errors.

24.1 How to Consume RESTful APIs Using Python

Making HTTP Requests Using the requests Library

The **requests** library in Python is a simple and elegant way to send HTTP requests and handle responses. It abstracts much of the complexity of interacting with APIs, making it a go-to choice for most Python developers when dealing with RESTful APIs.

Installing requests Library

First, ensure that you have the **requests** library installed. You can install it via pip if it's not already installed:

```bash
pip install requests
```

Making Basic GET Requests

The simplest API request is a **GET** request, which is used to retrieve data from a server. Here's an example of making a **GET** request to a public API, such as the **JSONPlaceholder** API:

```python
import requests

# Make a GET request to the JSONPlaceholder API
response = requests.get('https://jsonplaceholder.typicode.com/posts')

# Check if the request was successful (status code 200)
if response.status_code == 200:
    print("Request was successful!")
    print(response.text)   # The raw response content
else:
    print("Failed to fetch data:", response.status_code)
```

In this example:

- **requests.get()** sends a GET request to the specified URL.

- **response.status_code** contains the HTTP status code returned by the server (e.g., 200 means success, 404 means not found).

- **response.text** gives you the raw response body as a string.

Making POST, PUT, and DELETE Requests

For APIs that support data manipulation, you can make other types of HTTP requests such as **POST**, **PUT**, and **DELETE**.

Example of POST Request (Creating a New Resource):

```python
python

url                                            =
'https://jsonplaceholder.typicode.com/posts'
payload = {
    'title': 'foo',
    'body': 'bar',
    'userId': 1
}

response = requests.post(url, json=payload)

if response.status_code == 201:
    print("Resource created successfully!")
```

289

```
    print(response.json())    # Parse the JSON
response
else:
    print("Failed    to    create    resource:",
response.status_code)
```

- **POST Request**: Used to send data to the server to create a new resource.
- **json=payload**: Automatically serializes the payload to JSON.

Example of PUT Request (Updating a Resource):

python

```
url                                        =
'https://jsonplaceholder.typicode.com/posts/1'
payload = {
    'id': 1,
    'title': 'foo',
    'body': 'updated content',
    'userId': 1
}

response = requests.put(url, json=payload)

if response.status_code == 200:
    print("Resource updated successfully!")
```

```
    print(response.json())    # Parse the JSON
response
else:
    print("Failed    to    update    resource:",
response.status_code)
```

Example of DELETE Request (Deleting a Resource):

```python
url                                          =
'https://jsonplaceholder.typicode.com/posts/1'

response = requests.delete(url)

if response.status_code == 200:
    print("Resource deleted successfully!")
else:
    print("Failed    to    delete    resource:",
response.status_code)
```

24.2 Handling Responses

Once you make an HTTP request, the server will respond with data, usually in **JSON** format for RESTful APIs. In this section, we will learn how to handle API responses in Python.

Parsing JSON Responses

The most common data format returned by APIs is **JSON**. Fortunately, the **requests** library makes it simple to parse JSON responses with the **.json()** method.

```python
import requests

url = 'https://jsonplaceholder.typicode.com/posts'
response = requests.get(url)

if response.status_code == 200:
    data = response.json()  # Parse the JSON response into a Python dictionary
    print(data[0])  # Print the first post
else:
    print("Failed to fetch data:", response.status_code)
```

- **response.json()**: This method parses the JSON response and converts it into a Python dictionary (or a list if the response is an array).

Handling Status Codes

Every HTTP request returns a **status code**, which indicates whether the request was successful or not. It's important to check the status code of a response before trying to parse the response body. Here's a breakdown of common status codes:

- **200**: OK (request was successful)
- **201**: Created (resource was successfully created)
- **400**: Bad Request (incorrect request, often due to missing or invalid parameters)
- **404**: Not Found (the requested resource does not exist)
- **500**: Internal Server Error (server-side issue)

Example of checking status codes:

```python
python

response                                          =
requests.get('https://jsonplaceholder.typicode.
com/posts')

if response.status_code == 200:
    print("Request was successful!")
    data = response.json()
    print(data[:3])  # Print the first 3 posts
elif response.status_code == 404:
    print("Resource not found!")
else:
```

```
print(f"Error: {response.status_code}")
```

Handling Errors

Sometimes, the request will fail due to network issues, invalid URLs, or server errors. You can handle these situations with **try-except** blocks to catch exceptions and handle them gracefully.

python

```
try:
    response = requests.get('https://jsonplaceholder.typicode.com/posts')
    response.raise_for_status()    # Raises HTTPError for bad responses (4xx or 5xx)

    data = response.json()
    print(data)
except requests.exceptions.HTTPError as http_err:
    print(f"HTTP error occurred: {http_err}")
except requests.exceptions.RequestException as err:
    print(f"Other error occurred: {err}")
```

In this example:

- **raise_for_status()** will raise an exception if the response status code indicates an error (e.g., 404 or 500).

- **`requests.exceptions.RequestException`** catches all exceptions related to network issues, invalid URLs, etc.

24.3 Handling Query Parameters and Custom Headers

Sometimes, APIs require additional information in the form of **query parameters** or **custom headers**. Let's look at how to handle these with **requests**.

Sending Query Parameters

Query parameters are added to the URL to filter or modify the request. For example, you can filter posts by user ID.

python

```
url                                    =
'https://jsonplaceholder.typicode.com/posts'
params = {'userId': 1}   # Query parameter to
filter posts by userId

response = requests.get(url, params=params)

if response.status_code == 200:
    data = response.json()
    print(data)   # Print posts for userId 1
else:
```

```
print("Failed        to        fetch        data:",
response.status_code)
```

- **params=params**: Sends the query parameters as part of the URL.

Sending Custom Headers

Some APIs require custom headers, like **Authorization tokens** or **Content-Type** headers.

python

```
url                                              =
'https://jsonplaceholder.typicode.com/posts'
headers = {
    'Authorization': 'Bearer your_token_here',
    'Content-Type': 'application/json'
}

response = requests.get(url, headers=headers)

if response.status_code == 200:
    data = response.json()
    print(data)
else:
    print(f"Failed        to        fetch        data:
{response.status_code}")
```

- **headers=headers**: Sends custom headers with the request. Headers are typically used for **authentication, content-type specification**, and **rate-limiting** information.

Summary of Key Concepts

In this chapter, we covered how to consume **RESTful APIs** in Python using the **requests** library. The key concepts include:

- **Making HTTP Requests**: Using `requests.get()`, `requests.post()`, `requests.put()`, and `requests.delete()` to interact with APIs.
- **Handling API Responses**: Parsing JSON data with `.json()`, checking status codes to handle success or failure, and using `raise_for_status()` to raise exceptions for error codes.
- **Error Handling**: Using **try-except** blocks to handle exceptions like network issues or invalid responses.
- **Handling Query Parameters and Headers**: Sending query parameters using `params` and adding custom headers with `headers` for authentication and content-type specification.

Consuming APIs effectively is an essential skill for integrating external services and interacting with third-party systems. By mastering these concepts, you can efficiently interact with APIs, retrieve data, and handle errors or issues gracefully. In the next chapters, we'll dive into advanced techniques for optimizing API consumption and working with complex API systems.

CHAPTER 25

SCALING YOUR API

As your API grows and gains more users, you will need to ensure it can handle increased traffic without sacrificing performance. **Scaling** is the process of optimizing your API so that it can handle more requests, more data, and higher concurrency efficiently. In this chapter, we'll discuss strategies for **scaling Flask** and **Django applications**, covering both horizontal and vertical scaling techniques to ensure your APIs remain performant under heavy loads.

25.1 Scaling Flask Applications

Flask is a lightweight micro-framework, which makes it easy to get started with API development. However, when traffic increases, Flask may not be able to handle high volumes of requests without additional setup. To scale a Flask application, there are several techniques that can be implemented:

1. Vertical Scaling (Increasing Server Resources)

Vertical scaling involves adding more resources (CPU, RAM) to your current server to handle more requests.

- **Increase CPU and RAM**: If your API is running on a single machine, you can start by increasing its CPU and memory capacity. This helps handle more requests at once, especially if your app performs CPU-intensive tasks.

However, vertical scaling has limitations because there's a physical cap to how much you can increase the capacity of a single machine.

2. Horizontal Scaling (Adding More Servers)

Horizontal scaling, or **scaling out**, involves adding more servers to distribute the load. This is often the preferred method for large-scale applications. You can use a **load balancer** to distribute traffic across multiple instances of your Flask application.

- **Set Up Multiple Flask Instances**: Deploy multiple instances of your Flask application to run on different servers or containers. Each instance handles a portion of the incoming traffic.
  - Example: If you're using **Docker**, you can scale out your Flask app across multiple containers.
- **Use a Load Balancer**: A **load balancer** (e.g., **NGINX**, **HAProxy**) sits between users and your Flask instances, distributing requests evenly across the instances. This

helps balance traffic and improves redundancy in case one instance fails.

3. Use WSGI Servers for Concurrent Requests

Flask itself is not designed to handle multiple concurrent requests efficiently. It relies on **WSGI servers** like **Gunicorn** or **uWSGI** to manage multiple threads and handle concurrent requests.

- **Gunicorn**: A popular choice for deploying Flask applications, **Gunicorn** can spawn multiple worker processes to handle requests concurrently.

  Example command to run Flask with Gunicorn:

  bash

  ```
  gunicorn -w 4 app:app
  ```

  The -w 4 flag tells Gunicorn to spawn 4 worker processes, improving the app's ability to handle multiple requests at once.

4. Caching for Improved Performance

To reduce the load on your database and improve response times, you can implement caching strategies. **Redis** or **Memcached** are commonly used to cache frequently accessed data.

301

- **Cache API Responses**: For frequently requested data, you can cache responses to avoid making the same database queries repeatedly.

Example: Use **Flask-Cache** to cache API responses.

```bash
pip install Flask-Caching
python
```

```python
from flask import Flask
from flask_caching import Cache

app = Flask(__name__)
cache = Cache(app, config={'CACHE_TYPE': 'simple'})

@app.route('/data')
@cache.cached(timeout=50)
def get_data():
    return "Cached Data"
```

5. Use a Database Cluster

When scaling horizontally, your database can become a bottleneck. Use a **database cluster** to distribute database queries across multiple servers. You can use database replication, sharding, or distributed databases like **Cassandra** or **MongoDB** to handle increased load.

- **Read-Write Splitting**: Use a master-slave setup where write operations are sent to the master database, and read operations are distributed across slave databases.

6. Asynchronous Task Queue with Celery

For long-running tasks (e.g., email notifications, data processing), use an asynchronous task queue like **Celery** with **Redis** or **RabbitMQ**. Offload tasks to workers, allowing Flask to respond to API requests immediately without waiting for these tasks to finish.

25.2 Scaling Django Applications

Django is a more feature-rich framework than Flask and is designed to handle larger applications. However, as traffic increases, Django applications also need to be scaled. Let's look at how to scale Django applications effectively.

1. Vertical Scaling (Increasing Server Resources)

Like Flask, Django can also benefit from vertical scaling by increasing server resources. Start by upgrading your server's CPU, RAM, and storage. This helps improve response times and allows the server to handle more requests simultaneously.

2. Horizontal Scaling (Adding More Servers)

Horizontal scaling is essential for handling increased traffic. By deploying multiple instances of your Django application behind a load balancer, you can distribute traffic across servers and improve redundancy.

- **Using NGINX or HAProxy for Load Balancing**: A **load balancer** distributes incoming requests evenly across multiple Django instances. In a production environment, you typically set up a **reverse proxy** with **NGINX** or **HAProxy**.

  NGINX Example:

  ```nginx
  nginx

  upstream django {
      server 192.168.1.101:8000;
      server 192.168.1.102:8000;
  }

  server {
      location / {
          proxy_pass http://django;
      }
  }
  ```

3. Use WSGI Servers for Concurrency

Django uses **WSGI servers** like **Gunicorn, uWSGI**, or **Daphne** (for **asynchronous** views) to handle concurrent requests. These servers allow Django to spawn multiple worker processes, making it capable of handling many requests simultaneously.

Example command to run Django with **Gunicorn**:

```bash
bash
```

```bash
gunicorn --workers=4 myproject.wsgi:application
```

4. Caching in Django

Django provides built-in support for caching. Caching reduces the load on your database and speeds up response times. You can use **Memcached** or **Redis** for caching.

1. **Database Query Caching**: Cache frequently accessed query results using Django's cache framework.
2. **Page Caching**: Cache entire views or parts of views using Django's `cache_page` decorator.

```python
python
```

```python
from django.views.decorators.cache import cache_page
```

```
@cache_page(60 * 15)   # Cache the view for
15 minutes
def my_view(request):
    # view logic
    return                 render(request,
'template.html')
```

3. **Template Fragment Caching**: Cache specific parts of a template.

```
django
```

```
{% load cache %}
{% cache 600 my_cache_key %}
    <div>{{ expensive_data }}</div>
{% endcache %}
```

5. Database Optimization

A common bottleneck in large-scale applications is the **database**. To scale Django, you need to optimize your database for high traffic.

- **Database Indexing**: Use database indexes on frequently queried fields to speed up searches.
- **Read Replicas**: Set up **read-only replicas** of your database to distribute read traffic.
- **Database Sharding**: Split data across multiple databases based on specific criteria (e.g., user ID ranges).

6. Asynchronous Task Queue with Celery

Just like with Flask, offload long-running tasks to background workers in Django using **Celery**. This prevents blocking the main thread while Django processes long tasks like sending emails or generating reports.

1. **Set up Celery with Django**:

   bash

   ```bash
   pip install celery redis
   ```

2. **Configure Celery**:

   tasks.py:

   python

   ```python
   from celery import shared_task
   import time

   @shared_task
   def long_running_task():
       time.sleep(10)
       return "Task Completed!"
   ```

3. **Start Celery Worker**:

   bash

307

```
celery -A your_project_name worker --
loglevel=info
```

7. Database Connection Pooling

Use connection pooling to manage database connections more efficiently and reduce overhead. Tools like **pgbouncer** for PostgreSQL can be used to manage the number of database connections in a Django application.

25.3 Additional Considerations for Scaling

1. Auto-scaling and Cloud Infrastructure

In cloud environments (e.g., AWS, Google Cloud, Azure), you can set up **auto-scaling** to automatically increase or decrease the number of application instances based on the traffic load. This helps ensure your application can handle spikes in traffic without manual intervention.

2. Service Discovery

As you scale your API across multiple instances or containers, you might need a **service discovery** mechanism to ensure that your services can find and communicate with each other. **Consul** and **Eureka** are common tools used for service discovery.

3. Distributed Tracing and Monitoring

To manage and troubleshoot your distributed system, consider implementing **distributed tracing** using tools like **Jaeger** or **Zipkin**. These tools allow you to track requests across multiple services, giving you better insights into performance bottlenecks and error hotspots.

4. API Gateway

An **API Gateway** can act as a reverse proxy to route requests to the appropriate microservices, manage rate limiting, and handle authentication. This simplifies the API management and scaling process.

Summary of Key Concepts

In this chapter, we covered:

- **Scaling Flask applications** by using techniques such as vertical scaling, horizontal scaling with load balancing, using WSGI servers, caching, and using asynchronous task queues with Celery.
- **Scaling Django applications** through similar methods, with additional strategies like database replication, query

optimization, caching, and asynchronous tasks with Celery.

- **Best practices for scaling**, including auto-scaling in the cloud, service discovery, and using an API Gateway.

Scaling your application is crucial as traffic increases. By applying these techniques, you can ensure that both Flask and Django APIs can handle higher loads, provide better performance, and maintain reliability under heavy traffic. In the next chapters, we will explore securing APIs and best practices for deploying them to production environments.

CHAPTER 26

VERSIONING, DEPRECATION, AND API LIFECYCLE MANAGEMENT

As APIs evolve, it becomes crucial to manage the API's versions, handle deprecation gracefully, and ensure smooth transitions for users. This chapter covers essential concepts such as **API versioning**, **deprecating old endpoints**, and effectively managing the **API lifecycle** to maintain backward compatibility and a smooth user experience throughout updates.

26.1 Managing API Versions

Why API Versioning is Important

API versioning allows you to introduce changes to your API without breaking existing client applications. APIs evolve over time as you add new features, make improvements, or fix bugs. However, changes to the API (such as removing endpoints or changing data formats) may break the consumers of the API who rely on the older behavior. Therefore, versioning is essential for maintaining **backward compatibility**.

Common Techniques for Handling API Versioning

There are several approaches to versioning APIs. Each approach has its pros and cons, and choosing the right strategy depends on the nature of your application and how frequently you plan to introduce breaking changes.

1. **URI Path Versioning** (Most Common)
   o The API version is included as part of the endpoint URL.
   o Example:

   bash

   ```
   https://api.example.com/v1/users
   https://api.example.com/v2/users
   ```

   o **Pros**: Simple, easy to understand, and doesn't require additional configuration.
   o **Cons**: Can lead to URL clutter and requires careful planning for backward compatibility.

2. **Query Parameter Versioning**
   o The version is specified in the query string.
   o Example:

   bash

```
https://api.example.com/users?versi
on=1
https://api.example.com/users?versi
on=2
```

- o **Pros**: More flexible and can keep the same endpoint structure.
- o **Cons**: Can become confusing for clients and doesn't make it obvious which version of the API they're interacting with.

3. **Accept Header Versioning (Content Negotiation)**
   - o The version is specified in the request's **Accept** header.
   - o Example:

   ```bash
   ```

   ```
   Accept:
   application/vnd.example.v1+json
   ```

   - o **Pros**: Clean URLs, and allows for multiple versions of the API to exist under the same endpoint.
   - o **Cons**: Can be more complex for consumers, requiring them to specify headers correctly.

4. **Custom Header Versioning**
   - o The API version is included in a custom header (e.g., `X-API-Version`).

o   Example:

```bash
X-API-Version: 1
```

o   **Pros**: Allows flexibility in the request URL, keeping it clean.

o   **Cons**: Requires clients to be aware of and include the custom header in their requests.

Best Practices for Versioning

- **Start with a clear versioning strategy**: Decide upfront how you'll handle versions and document it clearly in your API documentation.

- **Increment only when necessary**: Use **semantic versioning** (major.minor.patch) and increment versions only when necessary, e.g., breaking changes increase the major version.

- **Avoid unnecessary breaking changes**: Keep backward compatibility as long as possible. This can be achieved by maintaining support for deprecated versions for a reasonable period.

- **Document changes clearly**: Always provide release notes that detail what has changed in each version, what has been deprecated, and what's coming in future versions.

314

26.2 Deprecating Old Endpoints

What Does Deprecating an API Endpoint Mean?

Deprecating an API endpoint means that it will no longer be maintained or updated, and it is recommended that users transition to a newer version of the API. Deprecation doesn't mean immediate removal — the endpoint is typically still functional, but developers are encouraged to migrate to the newer API version.

Best Practices for Deprecating API Endpoints

1. **Announce Deprecation Early**
   o **Notify users** well in advance of the deprecation. Provide a timeline and clear instructions on how to migrate to the new version.
   o Announce the deprecation through multiple channels such as email, the API documentation, and via HTTP headers.

2. **Mark Endpoints as Deprecated in Responses**
   o When an endpoint is deprecated, include a warning in the API response headers.
   o Example:

```http
```

```
HTTP/1.1 200 OK
```

```
X-API-Warning:    This    endpoint   is
deprecated and will be removed in the
next version.
```

3. **Provide a Clear Migration Path**
   o Provide detailed instructions on how to migrate to the newer version, such as endpoint changes, parameter changes, or response format modifications.
   o Include code samples and updates to ensure a smooth migration.

4. **Maintain Backward Compatibility (for a Period)**
   o Keep the deprecated endpoints functioning for a defined period (e.g., 6 months to 1 year) after announcing the deprecation, allowing users time to transition.

5. **Remove Deprecated Endpoints Gradually**
   o After the deprecation period, remove the endpoint in a future release. Communicate this final removal clearly in the release notes.
   o Example of a phased deprecation:
      ▪ **Phase 1**: Mark endpoint as deprecated (add warnings to responses).
      ▪ **Phase 2**: Disable new features or updates for the deprecated endpoint.
      ▪ **Phase 3**: Remove the endpoint entirely.

Example of Deprecating an Endpoint in Flask

python

```python
@app.route('/v1/old_endpoint', methods=['GET'])
def old_endpoint():
    response = {
        "message": "This endpoint is deprecated
and will be removed in the next version."
    }
    response.headers['X-API-Warning']   =   'This
endpoint is deprecated'
    return jsonify(response), 200
```

Example of Deprecating an Endpoint in Django

python

```python
from rest_framework.response import Response
from rest_framework.decorators import api_view

@api_view(['GET'])
def old_endpoint(request):
    response = {
        "message": "This endpoint is deprecated
and will be removed soon."
    }
    response['X-API-Warning'] = 'This endpoint
is deprecated'
    return Response(response, status=200)
```

26.3 Handling API Lifecycle

Managing the entire lifecycle of an API, from **development** to **deprecation** and eventual **removal**, is essential to ensure smooth transitions, continued user adoption, and effective API versioning.

Managing the API Lifecycle

1. **Initial Release**:
   - o Begin with a stable version, clearly defining the version number and the features offered. Use semantic versioning (e.g., v1.0.0) to make it easy for developers to understand the versioning scheme.

2. **Continuous Improvement**:
   - o As your API evolves, release new versions that introduce new features, fix bugs, and improve performance. Each new version should be **backward compatible** whenever possible to minimize disruption for users.

3. **Documenting Changes (Release Notes)**:
   - o Every time you release a new version or update, provide **release notes**. These notes should highlight:
     - **New features**: Describe any new functionality added.

- **Breaking changes**: Clearly mark any changes that will break existing functionality.
- **Deprecation notices**: Announce deprecated endpoints or features.
- **Bug fixes and performance improvements**.

Example of a release note:

```markdown

## Version 2.0.0 - 2023-04-01

### New Features:
- Added user authentication via OAuth2.
- New endpoint `/v2/orders` for managing orders.

### Breaking Changes:
- The `/v1/orders` endpoint is deprecated and will be removed in the next version.

### Bug Fixes:
- Fixed issue with the `GET /v1/users` endpoint returning incorrect data.
```

4. **Deprecation Phase**:

o   As mentioned earlier, mark old endpoints as **deprecated** and announce a clear timeline for removal. Provide users with enough time to migrate to newer versions.

5. **End of Life (EOL) and Removal**:

o   After the deprecation period, remove the outdated API version. Ensure that users are informed well ahead of time and provide alternative solutions if necessary.

Tools for Managing the API Lifecycle

- **Swagger/OpenAPI**: Helps you manage API documentation automatically and keep track of different versions.
- **GitHub or GitLab**: For version control and managing releases.
- **CI/CD Pipelines**: Automate the release process, making it easier to deploy new versions.
- **Monitoring**: Use monitoring tools like **Prometheus** or **Datadog** to track how your users are interacting with your API. This helps you understand usage patterns and plan for future versions.

Summary of Key Concepts

In this chapter, we covered:

- **API versioning**: Explained different techniques such as **path versioning**, **query parameter versioning**, and **header versioning** to manage multiple versions of an API.

- **Deprecating old endpoints**: Provided best practices for deprecating API endpoints gracefully by announcing changes in advance, providing migration paths, and maintaining backward compatibility during the deprecation period.

- **Handling the API lifecycle**: Discussed the complete API lifecycle from initial release to versioning, documentation, deprecation, and removal, with a focus on maintaining a smooth transition for users.

Effective API versioning, deprecation, and lifecycle management ensure that your API evolves with minimal disruptions, enabling users to migrate seamlessly to newer versions and continue benefiting from your service. In the next chapters, we will explore deploying your APIs at scale and strategies for securing your API.

CHAPTER 27

CONCLUSION AND REAL-WORLD USE CASES

In this final chapter, we will recap the **key concepts** and **best practices** covered throughout the book. We'll also dive into some **real-world case studies** that demonstrate the practical applications of Python-based APIs, and conclude with **next steps** and suggested further learning paths to continue your journey in building robust, scalable APIs.

27.1 Review of Key Concepts and Best Practices

Throughout this book, we have explored the fundamental aspects of **building, consuming, and managing RESTful APIs** using Python, Flask, and Django. Here's a summary of the key concepts and best practices we covered:

1. Introduction to RESTful APIs

- **REST (Representational State Transfer)**: A popular architectural style for designing networked applications.
- **Core principles**: Stateless, client-server architecture, uniform interface, cacheability, and layered system.

2. Setting Up Your Development Environment

- **Installing Python** and configuring **virtual environments** to isolate project dependencies.
- **Choosing the right IDE** and setting up necessary dependencies (Flask, Django, and other libraries).

3. HTTP Methods and Status Codes

- Understanding common HTTP methods such as **GET, POST, PUT**, and **DELETE**, and their usage in APIs.
- Importance of **HTTP status codes** in communicating the outcome of requests (e.g., 200 for success, 404 for not found, 500 for internal server error).

4. Flask vs. Django for API Development

- **Flask**: A lightweight micro-framework for building APIs quickly, ideal for small to medium-sized projects.
- **Django**: A more feature-rich framework, perfect for building large-scale applications with built-in support for ORM, authentication, and admin panels.

5. API Authentication and Security

- **JWT (JSON Web Token)** and **OAuth2** for securing APIs and authenticating users.

- **Best practices** for securing API endpoints, protecting data, and handling sensitive information.

6. Error Handling and Validation

- Techniques for **error handling** in APIs to provide meaningful error messages and gracefully handle exceptions.
- **Input validation** to ensure that incoming data is in the expected format before processing.

7. API Versioning and Deprecation

- Best practices for managing **API versions** to ensure backward compatibility.
- **Graceful deprecation** of old endpoints with clear communication to users and a defined migration path.

8. Scaling Your API

- **Vertical and horizontal scaling** techniques for Flask and Django applications to handle increased traffic.
- Use of **load balancers, caching**, and **asynchronous task queues** (e.g., Celery) to optimize performance under high loads.

9. Monitoring and Logging

- **Logging** for tracking API usage and debugging errors in Flask and Django applications.
- **Monitoring** with tools like **Sentry**, **Datadog**, and **Prometheus** to track performance metrics and ensure uptime.

10. Building API Documentation

- Using **Swagger/OpenAPI** for generating **interactive API documentation** that allows users to explore and test endpoints.
- Best practices for keeping documentation up-to-date and clear for users.

11. Consuming APIs with Python

- Using the `requests` library to **consume RESTful APIs** in Python, handling responses, checking status codes, and parsing JSON data.

27.2 Real-World Case Studies

To demonstrate the concepts and techniques covered in this book, let's look at some **real-world use cases** of Python-based APIs.

1. Spotify API

- **Overview**: Spotify provides a RESTful API that allows developers to access its music catalog, user playlists, and playback features.
- **Key Concepts**: The API supports **OAuth2 authentication**, uses **rate limiting** to manage requests, and has various **versioning strategies** to ensure compatibility across multiple platforms.
- **Real-World Application**: Many third-party applications use the Spotify API to integrate music recommendations, playlists, and playback controls, demonstrating how a well-designed API can drive external ecosystem growth.

2. Stripe API

- **Overview**: Stripe provides an API for online payment processing, allowing businesses to handle payments securely.
- **Key Concepts**: The Stripe API is known for its **clean documentation**, **webhooks** for asynchronous notifications, and **versioning** to ensure backward compatibility with older versions of the API.
- **Real-World Application**: **E-commerce platforms** and **subscription services** integrate Stripe to process payments, showcasing the flexibility and scalability of Stripe's API in handling high transaction volumes.

326

3. Twilio API

- **Overview**: Twilio's API allows developers to send and receive text messages, make voice calls, and manage communication workflows.
- **Key Concepts**: The API uses **RESTful principles** and is designed with **scalability** in mind, integrating well with cloud services to handle large volumes of messages and calls.
- **Real-World Application**: Twilio is used by **businesses** for **customer support**, **two-factor authentication**, and **automated messaging systems**, illustrating how an API can streamline communication workflows.

4. OpenWeatherMap API

- **Overview**: OpenWeatherMap provides weather data through its API, including current conditions, forecasts, and historical data.
- **Key Concepts**: The API includes **versioning** and allows users to customize requests with **query parameters** to get specific weather data for different locations.
- **Real-World Application**: Weather apps and websites rely on OpenWeatherMap's API to provide real-time and forecasted weather information, making it a key service in various weather-driven applications.

5. GitHub API

- **Overview**: GitHub's API offers access to repositories, user data, issues, and more. It allows developers to interact programmatically with GitHub's platform.
- **Key Concepts**: The API uses **OAuth authentication**, and **rate limits** are implemented to ensure fair usage and prevent abuse.
- **Real-World Application**: **DevOps tools, CI/CD pipelines**, and **code review systems** integrate with the GitHub API, automating code deployment, and improving collaboration in development teams.

27.3 Next Steps in API Development

Now that you have a solid foundation in API development using Python, Flask, and Django, it's time to continue building your skills and applying what you've learned. Here are some suggested **next steps**:

1. Explore More Advanced API Concepts

- **GraphQL**: Learn about **GraphQL**, a query language for APIs that allows clients to request specific data in a more efficient manner than RESTful APIs.

- **WebSockets**: Implement **real-time communication** using WebSockets for live updates, notifications, and chat applications.
- **Rate Limiting and Throttling**: Understand how to implement more sophisticated **rate limiting** strategies to manage traffic and prevent abuse.
- **API Security**: Dive deeper into **OAuth2, JWT** authentication, and **API key management** to build secure APIs.

2. Contribute to Open-Source Projects

- **GitHub**: Contribute to open-source projects that rely on Python-based APIs. This will give you hands-on experience working with production-level codebases and collaborating with other developers.

3. Practice Building Full-Stack Applications

- **Integrate APIs with Frontend Frameworks**: Build **full-stack applications** using **React, Vue.js**, or **Angular** for the frontend and Python-based APIs (Flask or Django) for the backend.
- **Deploy Applications**: Learn how to **deploy** your Flask or Django applications using **Docker, Heroku, AWS**, or **Google Cloud**. Familiarize yourself with setting up **CI/CD pipelines** for automated deployment.

4. Performance Optimization

- **Database Optimization**: Learn how to optimize database queries for large-scale applications using techniques such as **indexing, query caching**, and **database sharding**.
- **Distributed Systems**: Understand the concepts behind **microservices** and **distributed systems**, and learn how to scale your applications to handle global traffic.

5. Stay Updated

- **Read Documentation**: Stay up-to-date with the latest best practices, frameworks, and libraries by regularly reading documentation and blogs from major platforms like **Django, Flask, FastAPI**, and **Swagger**.
- **Join Developer Communities**: Participate in online communities (e.g., StackOverflow, Reddit, GitHub discussions) to learn from others, share your knowledge, and ask questions when you face challenges.

Summary of Key Concepts

In this final chapter, we:

- **Reviewed the core concepts** of **API versioning, deprecation**, and **lifecycle management**, emphasizing

330

the importance of backward compatibility and clear migration paths.

- **Explored real-world case studies** where Python-based APIs have been successfully used to power various services, from payment gateways to communication platforms.

- Suggested **next steps** for continued learning, including exploring advanced API topics, contributing to open-source projects, and improving your skills in performance optimization and deployment.

By following the best practices outlined in this book and continuing to explore the vast ecosystem of tools and techniques available for API development, you will be well on your way to building robust, scalable, and secure APIs that can grow with your applications.

www.ingramcontent.com/pod-product-compliance
Lightning Source LLC
LaVergne TN
LVHW051430050326
832903LV00030BD/3013